I0484569

THE NEW WORLD OF NETWORKED THINKING

THE NEW WORLD OF NETWORKED THINKING

Peter A. Schuller

Copyright © 2015 Peter A. Schuller
All rights reserved.

ISBN-13: 9781517010782
ISBN-10: 1517010780

ACKNOWLEDGEMENT

This book took a long time to research, and along the way I benefitted from many conversation partners who helped focus my thinking and scientific inquiry. Thanks to one and all—too many to even remember—for your generosity of spirit.

I am particularly grateful for the conversations and insights from a few thoughtful scientists who read early drafts and provided valuable feedback. Dr. John Seibyl, MD, Dr. Ed Monico, MD, and especially Dr. Peter Olausson, PhD, who guided some of my thinking and offered feedback from his own research on the human brain's reward system.

Special thanks also to William Baskin, JD, who used his sharp legal mind and command of the English language to pick up all my errors and ambiguities in the last draft.

And last, but far from least, my deepest gratitude goes to my greatest and most enduring conversation partner and supporter, my wife Sharon. You hear so many people saying "I could not have done it without so and so" that it almost sounds trite, but in this case, it is literally true, I could not have written this book without her love and support.

TABLE OF CONTENTS

It seems like every time I pick up a science magazine or read an article online, it mentions the word "mystery". Scientists have historically shied away from the word, but lately it seems to define the nature of their work—physicists chasing the mysteries of Black Holes, Dark Matter, and Dark Energy; biologists trying to explain the mystery of how life began; neuroscientists probing the mysteries of human thought and how it emerges from the workings of some complex neural circuitry. It almost seems that today's scientist has undergone a metamorphosis, from that of a dogmatic researcher intent on proving a given hypothesis to a curious observer enjoying the challenges of solving the deep mysteries of our universe.

Perhaps the worm began to turn much earlier than the 21st century. So many of today's research techniques and plausible theories have been spawned since the advent of mega-computing, in part because the emergence of tremendous computational power made such theories testable. Arguably, mega-computing was made possible in the mid to late 20th century by the fortuitous work of Alan Turing and Claude Shannon. Shannon's Information Theory may have been the single most important development of 20th century science, even though few non-scientists seem to be familiar with it. For example, even though it remains somewhat of a *mystery*, especially at levels of physical reality that we are unable to observe, the organization of our known universe revolves around a fascinating set of systems dynamics involving energy, Information, randomness, self-organization, and entropy. And Information, as contemplated by Shannon's theory (and discussed in Chapter Two), provides the common denominator from which to analyze those critical phenomena.

The approach I have adopted in this book on "networked thinking" certainly relies on the principles of Information Theory, as well of those related to self-organization in complex systems. We know little about the universe that lies beyond our powers of observation, either because we lack the instruments to measure it or it exists beyond the dimensions of spacetime, but within our solar system we can find enough examples of self-organizing Information sets to pique our interest. There is plenty of work to do in just investigating the mysteries of self-organization in organic systems, evolutionary speciation, societal systems, human culture, and of course our own enigmatic human brain/mind.

It is a fun time to be a scientist, not only to grapple with mysteries of the universe but to proffer different theories on the what's, how's, and why's of 21st century human existence. What we have learned, and the knowledge we have developed from learning in the last 100 years of our history, is truly astounding. On the other hand, what we still do not understand is truly humbling. The more we embrace what we do not yet know, the more fun it is to think about what we might yet discover.

Of course, that will take patience. Our brains are fundamentally prediction machines that thrive on information, so our minds become anxious and impatient when they sense there is important information still to be gained. The assignment is not an easy one. Our brains are constantly scanning for patterns of *relevant* information, amid the chaos, and sometimes they "see" patterns that do not actually exist. Moreover, much of the information our brains seek in order to make predictions about the future is unavailable—sometimes there is simply too much information to be processed, as is true with chaotic systems like the weather. Other times, it is difficult to assess what is relevant, because of how widely dispersed the information is, as is often the case in trying to anticipate what communications may constitute the making of a real terrorist threat. So our brains want to predict a future that by definition cannot be predicted, and in response to that dilemma, our minds generate theories, in order to allay our angst.

Fortunately, we persevere, because that is our nature. We build upon the knowledge bases that we have acquired and cautiously seek to extrapolate, particularly with regard to the overarching dynamics of self-organizing complexity. We may not yet be able to identify the precise organizing principles of our universe, but we do know that the energy necessary to direct the unfolding complexity of organic life here on earth comes from our Sun, and we know precisely how the photons it emits work their magic.

As a systems scientist, I believe that life and work should be creative. It should be filled with challenge and mystery, not reducible to defined rules and standard responses. It should be innovative, demanding, and provocative. It should be, well, somewhat random and unpredictable, so as to leave room for human invention. I hope that the concept of networked thinking carries that spirit of generative discovery, fed by patient and relentless thirst for knowledge, guided by an open-minded embrace of the unknown, as we collectively continue to solve life's pressing puzzles, one piece at a time.

Our observable universe—not only what cosmologists and physicists can see, analyze, and understand, but also the experience we think of as "life"—has become markedly more complex, and complicated, with the passage of time.

To my mind, what is complex and what is complicated are separate and distinct phenomena. And because making distinctions is an important aspect of human existence, investigating the differences between "complex" and "complicated" seems like a good place to start a book on "networked thinking".

Complexity is one of the truly interesting features of life here on earth, beginning at its most fundamental organic level. Even the simplest free living cells (called pleuronoma) have the components, assemblies of information, and interdependent processes—including genes, RNA, protein-synthesizing machinery, and protein production mechanisms—that are endemic to complex biological systems. Several billion years of evolution have necessarily increased the complexity of such systems.

And that is the interesting thing about organic systems. According to the 2nd Law of Thermodynamics, systems are supposed to move toward entropy, or disorder, and *decrease* in complexity. While that "law" in theory applies only to "closed" systems, it is hard to find any completely closed systems, especially among the natural ones that exist here on earth. Accordingly, most complexity scientists deal with the 2nd Law of Thermodynamics by using the tools of statistical mechanics to analyze the nature of dynamics generally, and the dynamics of self-organizing systems in particular.

Life in our self-organizing solar system is all about the relationship among entropy, heat transfer, and complexity. The chemistry that drives the evolutionary processes of life on earth ultimately lowers the energy of the particular system in which that chemistry is taking place, thereby reducing the entropy within that system, while increasing the heat—and entropy—of the system's surroundings. The greater the heat loss within a given system, the greater the possibility for complexity. That is our world, and that is why life sustains itself here, becoming ever more complex in its systems dynamics, notwithstanding the 2nd Law of Thermodynamics.

Although there is much that we do not know about the dynamics of self-organization here on earth, especially with regard to the human brain system, we do know that the primary source of energy, and organizing principle, that gives rise to the emergence of life is our Sun—most particularly the countless photons that continually bombard our planet. In order to stave off the pull of entropy, a system must receive a continual injection of energy. This injection of energy, referred to as "Work" in systems science, comes primarily from the Sun's photons, which are carriers of both energy and Information. Photons bump electrons into higher energy orbits and catalyze the processes of energy and heat transfer that make it possible for systems to cool down, become more ordered, and increase in complexity over time. For example, photons are critical to the formation of key organic compounds, especially carotene and chlorophyll, which are fundamental to organic growth. And at the same time, being massless carriers of the electromagnetic force, these photons also have embedded in them the Information, as defined by Information Theory, that drives the mechanics of organic chemistry and molecular biology, the building blocks of self-organizing evolution.

So self-organization is enabled within our solar system because these photons, which arrive on earth in a range of energy frequencies and therefore contain different patterns of Information, perform the Work that reduces entropy and generates complex forms of order; and because all self-organizing systems necessarily become more complex with time, we live in a world of increasing complexity, notwithstanding the 2nd Law of Thermodynamics.

Moreover, thanks to these photons, and other still unidentified sources of Work producing energy and Information (perhaps embedded in quantum systems or the Zero Point Field), self-organizing organic systems here on earth can absorb considerable amounts of entropy. That capacity allows for the emergence of randomness within such systems, which, as discussed in Chapter One, is essential for generating new, adaptive ideas and strategies. All self-organizing systems are therefore necessarily complex *and* adaptive.

Most importantly for purposes of this book, these dynamics bear directly on both our understanding of the self-organizing human brain system and the approach we need to take in creating optimal models of organizational development, as discussed in Chapter Nine.

More broadly, what we now consider "complex" orients around the interrelationship of things, especially in systems. Complex Systems (or simply Complexity) Science occupies itself with identifying and analyzing organizing principles, rules, and law-like behaviors that explain how random elements take up different forms of order, then interact with each other to create something more than the sum of those elements. Complexity Science also tries to break down and analyze the way components of a system operate in circular cause and effect with each other (where causes become effects and vice versa), create certain systems dynamics such reinforcing and counterbalancing feedback systems, and even generate "emergent phenomena". In the science of complex systems, it is particularly important to distinguish detail complexity (the characteristic variables associated with systems components) from dynamic complexity (the number and nature of components in the system and how they interact in interdependent cause and effect relationships).

What is "complicated", on the other hand, may or may not be an inevitable aspect of modern life. We are, by evolutionary process, highly socialized animals, so over the 50,000 or so years that our species has lived within organized social structures, we have developed decidedly "complicated" sets of: 1) social rules, conventions, and mores; 2) psychological and emotional expectations; 3) thoughts and associated feelings; and 4) learned, conditioned responses. Within the industrialized world, our *complex* physical and social environments necessarily present each of us—and the different groups we belong to—with a very *complicated* set of options, choices, desires, and motivations. To meet the challenges of our complex world, our powerful brains and resourceful minds have learned how to contemplate the demands of our varied environments, make predictions about the consequences of our actions, and strategize about the changes we might implement to enhance our chances of survival, all of which seems inevitably to translate into some measure of complication.

Nevertheless, there is at least some element of choice involved in the distinctions between complexity and complication—complexity may be an inevitable aspect of modern life, but at least to some degree, we can decide how complicated we might allow our lives to become.

To better manage our lives within this increasingly complex and potentially complicated environment, we will need new tools and more sophisticated forms of intelligence; we must gain a better understanding of how our self-organizing human brain systems work, what our minds are like, and the capacities we possess for changing either of them. We will need to learn how to develop and live into what Carol Dweck calls "growth mindsets", leaving behind the "fixed mindsets" that have limited the breadth of our thinking and the full expanse of our intelligence. We will need to learn how to leverage the power of networks and genetic algorithms, which will allow us to experiment with existing information and knowledge bases, so as to generate new and better "ideas" for our evolutionary development, just as Nature has done with speciation for billions of years.

It is a bit of a challenge to be sure, but we already have many of the requisite tools and simply have not fully deployed them yet. Moreover, we may be about to enter a golden age of brain and gene research that would add a few things to our toolbox. For example, a group of bioengineers in Switzerland recently developed a system to translate human brain activity into electromagnetic fields that can trigger protein production in human cells, using optogenetic mechanisms. This approach opens up yet another avenue for investigating the complex interrelationship involving our thoughts, the dynamics of gene expression, and the effects they engender in our brains and bodies. Moreover, we are gaining better insights every day into the mechanics of epigenetics, a science that seeks to break down and analyze how genes respond to new information from both their internal and external environments. For humans, such information from the environment may be sourced in a whole range of socio-economic and cultural systems, or involve complex psychological and other mental phenomena.

It seems possible that the concept of "networked thinking" might help us better optimize the tools we have available to us already, given the tremendous capacities of our brains and the knowledge we have acquired to date about how things work in our universe. Networked thinking offers a process to engage in more expansive and innovative thinking, for both ourselves and our organizations. I derived the concept from a cross-disciplinary analysis of complex systems, network dynamics, Information Theory, and brain systems science.

With this cross-disciplinary scientific approach in mind, it strikes me that genius may be the art of rendering the complex simple, and as I am no genius, I have done my best to make my explanations of the concepts in this book as straightforward as possible, if not entirely simple. It was supposedly Einstein who said that "everything should be made as simple as possible, but not simpler", and that certainly applies to the theoretical construct that lies behind the whole concept of networked thinking. Toward that end, I have outlined this construct in the paragraphs that follow, as a preview to the substance of Chapters One through Seven.

Based on the last few decades of scientific research, it seems clear that we live in a fundamentally self-organizing universe, one that faithfully follows various "rules" and "laws" in the many processes by which order emerges from apparent chaos and randomness. The story of our universe appears to be one in which unorganized, seething fields of energy first manifest as chaotic systems, then develop into forms of predictable order, without any **centralized** process-producing mechanism. Using the principles of mathematics devised over time by observing these distributed processes, we are able to ascribe a host of probability profiles to the self-organizing systems of our universe, so that we can continue to get better at making predictions about the world we live in.

We think of these organizing "rules" and "laws"—for example, the "law" of gravity—as fixed and finite, but really they represent probabilistic patterns of activity or behavior that are so likely to happen as to be virtually guaranteed. Thanks to all our scientific disciplines and the tools of mathematics we have derived over centuries, we have been able to quantify many different probability sets and identify a wide range of "rules" that we can count on, within everything from quantum systems to the self-organizing dynamics of evolution. (In others, such as economic systems, such "rules" have proved to be more elusive!)

When we look at the varied dynamics of physical systems, a theory of self-organization has both compelling inductive and deductive support. Inductively, no other combination of theories provides a better explanation for the phenomenon of quantum decoherence or the organizing principles of countless complex adaptive systems that define life here on earth. Nothing else better explains the relativistic relationship Einstein identified between spacetime and matter, or the exquisite balance that exists within our known universe between order and randomness, readily observed within the "laws" of thermodynamics. From all that we know about the physics of energy and the various fields that exert their own influences (Higgs, weak and strong force, electromagnetism, etc.), we could not expect to find an observable universe of spacetime and matter that did not give rise to the decoherence of quantum systems, and we could not expect to encounter such decoherence without the presence of some underlying organizing principle.

Deductively, we find that many of the most relevant complex adaptive systems of our human existence world fit the model predicted by the mechanics of self-organization. Self-organization necessarily involves not only predictable patterns of self-assembly but essential systems elements such as feedback and balancing systems, goal-oriented adaptation, and dynamic cause and effect interactions. We can observe all of these elements within not only the natural physical systems of our solar system but our man-made social and cultural systems as well.

Given this underlying premise of self-organization, the rest of the theoretical construct, which is fleshed out in Parts I and II of the book, is summarized below and graphically represented in Figure 1:

1. All forms of energy and matter, as well as the systems they organize into, are defined by the Information they contain. ("Information" is capitalized here and throughout the book to indicate that it refers to the term as it is conceptualized in and contemplated by Information Theory.)

2. At its moment of Singularity, just prior to the event we refer to as the "Big Bang", our universe contained the maximum amount of Information; immediately after the Big Bang, the resultant fields of random energy forms began to self-organize, through a process by which energy and Information in chaotic systems eventually becomes and remains ordered, while remaining subject to the disordering influences of entropy; self-organizing systems eventually emerge from the process by which energy and Information are constantly injected into such systems to perform the "Work" necessary to stave off the relentless effects of entropy and generate order.

3. Self-organizing systems we observe here on earth rely on both "Random Information" and "Ordered Information", using the 1) predictive statistical "rules" embedded in Ordered Information to maintain stable growth and 2) programming of "genetic algorithms" to manipulate Random Information and generate new "ideas".

4. Complex adaptive systems, whether self-organizing or not, generate "emergent phenomena" that add adaptive capabilities and tools, which can process both Random Information and Ordered Information so as to expand the type of adaptive mechanisms available to these systems; in some cases, especially with regard to the human brain system and emergent mind, these emergent phenomena add new levels of organization to the system.

5. Complex adaptive systems rely heavily on Information synthesis and feedforward/feedback systems to continually operationalize the Information flowing through the systems, so as to improve the systems' predictive mechanisms and adjust their goals and objectives. ("Synthesized Information")

6. Networks self-organize, usually in "Small World" networks, within these complex adaptive systems in order to most efficiently process and distribute Synthesized, Ordered, and Random Information within these systems, while at the same time remaining resilient to network failure or external attack on the network.

7. The human brain is a self-organizing, complex adaptive system that uses Ordered, Random, and Synthesized Information, as well as genetic algorithms, emergent phenomena such as consciousness, and the dynamics of Small World networks to generate "intelligent" thought and decision making.

8. Networked thinking leverages many of these principles to potentially generate both a higher order of emergent human intelligence and a methodology for optimizing strategic thinking and decision making.

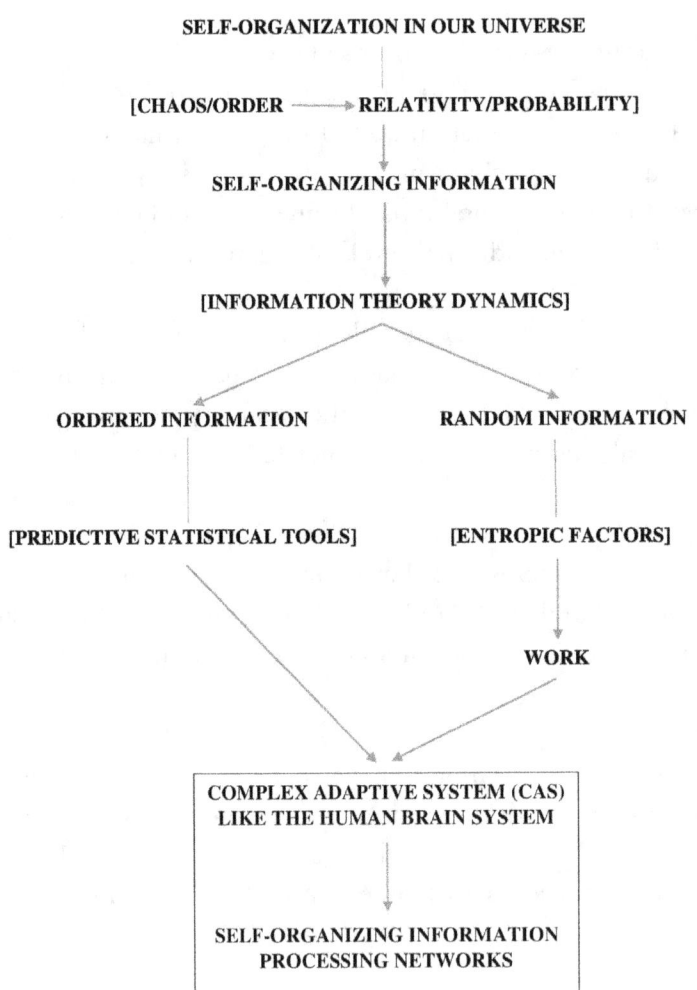

SELF-ORGANIZING AND COMPLEX ADAPTIVE SYSTEMS DYNAMICS

SELF-ORGANIZATION IN OUR UNIVERSE

[CHAOS/ORDER ⟶ RELATIVITY/PROBABILITY]

SELF-ORGANIZING INFORMATION

[INFORMATION THEORY DYNAMICS]

ORDERED INFORMATION   **RANDOM INFORMATION**

[PREDICTIVE STATISTICAL TOOLS]   **[ENTROPIC FACTORS]**

WORK

**COMPLEX ADAPTIVE SYSTEM (CAS)
LIKE THE HUMAN BRAIN SYSTEM**

**SELF-ORGANIZING INFORMATION
PROCESSING NETWORKS**

So, it all starts with the concepts of Information Theory and self-organization, but in the end, it's all about the dynamics of complex adaptive systems and networks. In the ensuing chapters, I will go into more detail on some key points about self-organization, Information Theory, complex adaptive systems, emergent phenomena, and networks. I will not go into such detail regarding genetic algorithms, because, for one, it would require a somewhat technical explanation, but also because for our purposes here, we need only deal with the general mechanics of genetic algorithms and how they apply globally to the adaptive dynamics of complex systems and networked thinking. So I will briefly address that subject here.

By way of explaining those general mechanics, genetic algorithms are Nature's preferred method of generating new "ideas" for adaptive fitness, using the clever process of gene replication, mutation, fitness testing, and selection. The genetic algorithms themselves are used to generate various possible "ideas" and test their fitness. By leveraging the use of random mutations that occur in individual genes or gene sequences, Nature can generate many different, and often fast-acting, testable potential solutions to problems or challenges that may confront a given species within its particular environment. Nature also uses genetic algorithms to generate new "ideas" that may have nothing to do with solving pending challenges and much more to do with creating entirely novel and interesting phenomena that *might* provide a given species with a competitive advantage when environmental conditions change at some later date. It is sort of Nature's way of continuing to "think out of the box", and it is very relevant to our pursuit of networked thinking.

The primary reason this adaptive and creative trick works so well is the leverage that is generated by the *network* structure of genomes and how genes are expressed, in response to some type of information input. In general, whether deployed in gene networks, computer programs, or the human brain system, genetic algorithms use simple statistical rules to keep testing the adaptive utility of a given feature or new "idea". Networked thinking seeks to replicate this adaptive strategy, particularly by using the leverage generated within networked information sharing systems. Moreover, to work effectively, genetic algorithms must be deployed in complex adaptive systems and programs (computer or otherwise) that have robust feedback systems, which is also an element of networked thinking.

Genetic algorithms work particularly well within the information pro-cessing dynamics of the human brain system. Specifically, as they relate to the nature and power of the brain and networked thinking, genetic algorithms might be thought of as a mechanism that 1) begins with the "chunking" of data bits and patterns of information in disparate neural networks, 2) progresses to the identification and manipulation of "objects" by a discrete system located in the human mid-brain, 3) allows for the pro-cessing of Random Information, and 4) completes itself when the whole brain system reconfigures different patterns of information and allows the mind to generate new "ideas" from the "objects" that are available in the brain's memory systems. (As explained in Chapter Seven, the human brain system treats everything as an "object" and forms internal represen-tations of each such "object" in order to effectively compare, contrast, and associate these "objects", whether they are what our minds conceive as concrete and tangible or more elusive and intangible, like a concept or someone's subjective experience of something. To anchor this point, I will continue to put quotes around the word "object" when it is used in this context. I will also use "ideas" in quotes to signify all the forms of outputs from different applications of genetic algorithms, ranging from those generated by Nature in evolution to the many creative thoughts produced by the human mind.)

The creative genius of genetic algorithms is only one of many power-ful tools that defines our self-organizing, complex adaptive human brain system. It seems almost magical that so many billions of cells could not only self-assemble into a coherent information processing network but also form discrete, yet integrated systems that fulfill hundreds of com-plex functions. And on top of that, this complex adaptive system and network of networks also generates the entirely unique set of emergent phenomena we think of as human mind, consciousness, intelligence, will, intention, and thought, all of which can have a "top down" effect on the operational functionality of the underlying brain system, information processing networks, and self-organizing "software" programs within the mind. (Obviously, what makes this state of affairs particularly interesting is that such emergent phenomena are self-observed—in other words, we characterize and describe them using the very mind, intelligence, and thoughts we believe we are observing—maybe a little like those infinity pictures that repeat the same image within progressively smaller depic-tions of itself.)

The concept of human mind is necessarily elusive, and its character-istics are hard to catalogue. Based on all of my research, I am convinced that the human mind has aspects to it that lie beyond our comprehension and extend into "spaces" well beyond the mental landscape of our own consciousness. Countless theories abound about the nature of the human mind, and frankly I find most of them intriguing—whether framed in the context of quantum mechanics, Eastern and Western spirituality, or other rational constructs, it seems clear that the human mind has capaci-ties and characteristics that derive from sources beyond its connections to the human brain system. That said, in this book, I will refer to the human mind primarily in the context of how it emerges from the operational mechanics and functionality of the human brain system.

The concept of networked thinking I propose is founded on the idea that this emergent mind has two distinct aspects and sets of capabilities or tendencies. These two aspects of mind emerge from one or the other of two discrete systems in the brain—what I have termed "Default" and "Integrated". While the mind generated by the Default system may appear to operate somewhat independently of all other aspects of mind, the one that emerges from the Integrated system is by definition holistic and seeks to integrate the functional systems of the Default system without being governed by them. (Please note that this "Default system" should not to be confused with what is referred to in neuroscience circles as the "Default Mode Network", which involves a completely different concept.)

My approach hopefully gains credibility from the decades of research performed on Split-Brain patients, usually as a result of surgeries that elim-inate or reduce the connections between the brain's right and left hemi-spheres, in order to alleviate symptoms of severe epilepsy. Such research has established that each hemisphere of our brains has both redundant and somewhat unique, specialized systems, and each is therefore able to generate a "mind" that can "interpret" what is going on and report it in a way that "makes sense" to the conscious mind, even though it does not have access to all of the information being processed at the time in the other hemisphere. If such systemic and structural differences between the brain's hemispheres give rise to somewhat "independent" minds, there is no reason why two different aspects of mind could not also emerge from the two distinct operational systems of the brain.

My construct for both the human brain system and the emergent mind not only focuses on these two discrete systems but also adopts two distinct angles of analysis, using the lens of a "top down/bottom up" systems approach on the one hand and network science on the other. By now, it must be obvious that I refer to the "human brain *system*", rather than just the "brain". Part II of the book covers the essence of human brain systems dynamics and describes the particularities of the Default and Integrated systems. In *Thinking Fast and Slow,* Daniel Kahneman, the Nobel Prize-winning scientist who suggests a similar type of dualistic approach oriented around what he calls "System 1" and "System 2", opts for a "top down", empirical approach. While that construct helps us understand why we do and think as we currently do, it falls short of investigating how we might improve on our information processing and thinking, which requires a "bottom up" analysis of how: 1) various identified functional systems are networked together, and 2) "strong" emergent phenomena, such as the mind and the capacity to think, influence or even alter the structures and operations of the underlying brain system. Accordingly, I believe it is essential to undertake both a top down and bottom up analysis of our brain's Default and Integrated systems, and the emergent phenomena they generate.

The second perspective, which is informed by network science (covered in Chapter Three), revolves around both the dynamics of self-organizing networks and the mechanics of Information Theory. To process and distribute the Information that performs entropy reducing Work, self-organizing networks must attain the highest levels of efficiency, without sacrificing too much continuity, stability, or resilience to internal failure and external attack. Efficiency in this case essentially means *performance* divided by *cost.* Over the last two decades, network science has provided critical new insights on how real, self-organizing networks invariably adopt structures known as "Small World" in order to achieve the highest performance at the lowest cost, with the highest feasible levels of resiliency to failure and/or external attack.

Biologists and anatomists have known for some time that nervous systems, cells, and even molecules self-organize into Small World networks in order to efficiently exchange information and "communicate". But now we are discovering that ecologies, societies, food chains, rivers, epidemics, and even languages also use such sophisticated network structures to efficiently self-organize and process Information. Interestingly, Marios Koniaris and his colleagues at the National Technical University of Athens (Greece) have recently discovered that even the laws of the European

Union connect to each other in a sophisticated network structure of treaties, regulatory directives, international legal principles, and enacted legislation. (They analyzed 250,000 documents embedded in a network of over a million links, which, not surprisingly, were connected in a Small World network.)

Efficiency is also an issue in Information Theory, which offers two interesting perspectives that play a critical role in the development of networked thinking. The first of these perspectives relates to the tenets of Claude Shannon's originally conceived Information Theory (sometimes referred to as "Shannon Information Theory"), and the second involves the application of Shannon's theory to physical systems and is primarily driven by Ludwig Boltzmann's approach to statistical mechanics (sometimes referred to as "Boltzmann Information Theory").

Shannon Information Theory demonstrates how messages are communicated at various levels of certainty, based on how "redundant" they are and how much randomness, or "noise", they contain. Messages with high levels of certainty are considered very "redundant", which also means that considerable energy is required to both generate and transmit the Information contained within them. (The less redundancy is transmitted in a string of Information bits, the more room there is for Information from other messages, so Shannon basically was the first to devise a system to compress messages without eliminating the level of certainty required to successfully transmit any given message.)

Randomness embedded in messages, on the other hand, contains considerable "noise", which interferes with the effective transmission of a specific message but offers the possibility of generating important new bits of Information that allow systems to create innovative solutions and adapt. (Technically, in Information Theory, "noise" includes anything that corrupts the signal in a message, whether that involves irrelevant additions, straightforward error, random disturbances, distortions, or other forms of unpredictability. In this technical sense, "noise" is very relevant to how genes express and the human brain system operates, both of which regularly deal with all of these "noisy" occurrences. For example, within the dynamics of evolution, gene mutation leading to the emergence of new "ideas" occurs not just from copying errors but from the "noise" that invades the sequencing and expression of genes.

The human brain system traffics in all kinds of different messages, requiring that some, such as those transmitted back and forth between applicable brain systems and the body's endocrine systems, be very specific and certain, while allowing others, such as random thoughts, to be "noisier". Moreover, because it must conserve precious energy, the human brain system does not always have the luxury of sending completely redundant messages and often defaults to using its most exigent and energy-efficient information processing techniques, as discussed in Part II. To reinforce their efficiency, these information processing tools also take advantage of what Information Theory refers to as the Principle of Least Effort, which involves a formulaic approach to finding the right level of Information redundancy to insure accurate message transmittal without consuming unnecessary energy. Of course, the downside of this set of dynamics emerges when someone allows his or her entire brain system and thought processes to be governed by these "default" dynamics, and it is certainly not hard to find evidence today of human thinking that is governed by the principle and dynamics of "least effort"!

Equally importantly, Information Theory reveals a great deal about the information processing that takes place in our human brain systems, which are fundamentally geared to constantly seek out new, *relevant* information, in order to keep making better and better predictions. In this never-ending process of sifting through information for relevance, as well as continually discarding encoded information that is later found to be irrelevant, the human brain system has to sort through a great deal of the "noise" that is embedded in most of the messages it receives from its internal and external environments. Moreover, recognizing information that is relevant is primarily driven by the rules of statistical mechanics, applied to the brain system's existing predictions. As discussed in Chapter Two, Boltzmann Information Theory provides a means of training our brain systems to better recognize and sort through the "noise", identify information that can improve our predictive strategies, and enhance our capacity for networked thinking.

Finally, in PART III, I delve into the dynamics and practical mechanics of networked thinking and what I call "Knowledge Networks". Because the human brain is itself a complex, adaptive, and highly networked system, the thinking it produces represents yet another level of organizational structure, which both defines and affects the content of the emergent human mind, thanks to the top down influences of emergent phenomena in complex adaptive systems. When one factors in the 1) systems and network dynamics of the human brain system, 2) workings of the human mind, 3) effect of both randomized and ordered Information flowing through the brain and mind, 4) emergence of thoughts and their impact on the mind from which they emerge, and 5) interactive effects generated by an individual's brain system and mind on the brain systems and minds of others, a great deal of both detail and dynamic complexity emerges. We have to find a way to cut through all that complexity, and as detailed in Chapter Eight, I think we must use network science to do so.

Networked thinking has both individual and collective facets to it. Chapter Eight discusses the keys to becoming individually more effective, intelligent thinkers, while Chapter Nine takes on the different possibilities for using networked thinking to build better information and knowledge sharing systems, greater collective intelligence, and new approaches to organizational development, using network science to design and operate effective Knowledge Networks. Knowledge Networks involve the complexity and challenges of sharing both information and knowledge in a way that optimizes organizational innovation and development.

As such, Knowledge Networks necessarily include the added element of human agency, and once we introduce human agency into the picture, both systems and network dynamics necessarily become unavoidably more difficult to sort out. Fortunately, we can use network science to work through such complexity and suggest effective strategies for managing knowledge transfer and generating innovation. Both agent-based systems and personal networks are affected by similar elements of personality, preferences, and other human characteristics that draw us toward or push us away from each other, thereby complicating the communication landscape and influencing group behavior. The good news is that such agent-based systems and personal networks also possess parallel reinforcing (feedback based) dynamics, which may make it easier to understand the mechanics of Knowledge Networks, networked thinking, and emergent collective intelligence.

All of which brings us back to the distinction between "complex" and "complicated". In everyday life, complexity and complication cross over. Complexity necessarily generates high levels of cause and effect interrelationship among the components of a system, and it is no secret that the human brain system struggles mightily (and often fails) to sort out the countless events of cause and effect in our daily lives, which makes managing them quite complicated. For example, because of the time lag that often occurs between a cause and its apparent effect, such as when the stock market reacts a full two weeks after a few major port strikes have significantly slowed the shipping of a commodity that is vital to a certain major industry, our brain systems and minds have trouble figuring out precisely what data and information they should pay attention to in order to assess the cause and effect dynamics at play and adjust their strategic predictions. And then when it turns out that we have focused on the wrong information, we often make decisions that just further complicate matters and require even more attention and difficult decisions to rectify the situation. The housing bubble working up to 2007 comes to mind, as does the word "complicated" for what happened shortly thereafter!

At the end of the day, however, the interplay of complexity and complication in our 21st century lives is also what epitomizes the true uniqueness of human intelligence and offers us the best hope of expanding that intelligence even further. Why? Because it is precisely the *adaptive* complexities of the human brain system that give rise to our strategic minds, generate the many different forms of our intelligence, and provide us with the innate capacity to learn, all of which lies at the heart of networked thinking.

Fortunately, the human brain system is predisposed toward networked thinking, and we only need to learn how to take better advantage of what we already know how to do. 50,000 years ago, it appears that we survived and thrived as a species, where the Neanderthals did not, because we were just a little bit better at forming collaborative networks. Now, with some measure of awareness, intention, strategy, and practice, we can learn to leverage our native capacity for network thinking and in doing so even begin to reorganize the structures of our brains, most likely in ways that can be passed on, genetically and epigenetically, to future generations of increasingly capable networked thinkers.

There is every reason to believe that we can expand our intelligence and become more effective thinkers and decision makers. Whatever else might be said about the human species, in terms of its social development, morality, and evolutionary "progress", there is no doubt about the uniqueness of our intelligence, compared to that of all other species. We have long since escaped the boundaries of any localized physical environment and the need to adapt to changes within it, having learned how to cool and heat many of our workplaces and travel from one eco-system to another in mere hours. For better or worse, we have also distinguished ourselves from all other species in our level of self-awareness, consciousness, and intentionality, although in all fairness we fall short as a species of the self-reflective consciousness, concern for others, and efforts at collaboration that we are eminently capable of, given what our brain systems are actually hardwired to deliver. Whatever the collective shortcomings of our species, we have sharpened the skills of language and communication, laid down the rules of social convention, and built extensive enough scientific knowledge bases to invent new communication frontiers like the Internet and Web, so as to efficiently share our know-how and continue to become collectively more intelligent. And yet, we are capable of so much more.

Fortunately, in the 21st century, it does seem that we are finally at least beginning to sober ourselves to the reality of our complex and complicated world. Most of us struggle to avoid being overwhelmed by it, and though we often run from change, we do understand that change is necessarily a part of our existence. We also understand that short-term fixes are no substitute for meaningful long-term solutions to the challenges of our complex and complicated world. Long term, we need to find a whole new way of being—one that begins with a different perspective on the nature of our brain systems and our capacity for proactively rewiring them.

As we begin this sobering process, we will collectively have to learn the tendencies of our complex adaptive brain systems, which, if left to their own devices, will adopt the path of least resistance (and smallest expenditure of energy), defaulting into simplistic, linear, associative computation and thought. We will need to understand the nature of our minds, our consciousness, and how we can learn to consistently move beyond that default oriented system of thinking. We will need to understand the dynamics of networks and how networked thinking can open up an entirely new process of idea creation and decision making. The challenge is daunting to some, but the rewards are potentially immense.

Those rewards include not only making us more intelligent but transforming our very nature, because, among other things, networked thinking will make us more "other oriented" in our perspectives and behaviors. We will collaborate more easily and align our minds more cohesively, within our own mental spaces and with the minds of others, in our collective efforts to deal with the challenges of 21st century life, and beyond. A human culture that glorifies the achievements of its "great" individuals, whatever their disciplines, at the expense of the collective's basic welfare, cannot sustain itself indefinitely, because doing so defies the dynamics of self-organization.

Although I would never claim it as a motivation for writing this book, I hope that embracing the concept of networked thinking might also provide a different perspective for our study of the human brain system, which has seemingly become a popular project lately. At present, the discipline of neuroscience appears to be stuck in some form of virtual limbo, where reductionist methods ignore the dynamics of the complex adaptive brain system (especially emergence), and constructionist approaches focus on analyzing the dynamics of molecular and cellular biology, while failing to provide a holistic view of the entire system. Even the ambitious WU-Minn-HCP Consortium's "Connectome" project, which appears to take a more holistic, network-centric approach, has its limitations. All the while, the search is on for a theory that describes the type of "middleware" that the human brain system uses to integrate its entire range of physiological mechanisms and vast number of emergent phenomena, cognitive capacities, dynamic behaviors, thoughts, and feelings. Perhaps the key to developing that theory lies in the marriage of complexity science and network science, and perhaps the investigation of how we might enhance our capacity for networked thinking will send us down a useful path in pursuing such a theory. Nothing ventured, nothing gained.

PART I—SELF-ORGANIZATION, INFORMATION, AND NETWORKS

1

OUR SELF-ORGANIZING UNIVERSE

Self-organizing Systems

When we look around our observable universe, especially the small sections that we can probe with telescopes and space probes, we find one particular, truly amazing feature—the presence of a sentient, self-aware being. Though our universe could contain thousands, if not millions, of planets with the capacity to sustain some sort of organic life and other forms of sentient beings, we humans are completely different than anything else we have been able to observe in our solar system. It is of course possible that our "sentience" is an illusion and that we cannot in fact "observe" our own sentient nature any more than quantum superpositions can be observed without collapsing into particular systems. And it is also possible that other phenomena here on earth, organic or not, have some form of quantum or holographic consciousness that is far more spectacular than human self-awareness and sentience. But for what we can say now, humans alone are aware of their own existence, the dynamics of their environment, and the willful power of their own minds. (Not to mention the possibility that we do have a higher form of quantum or holographic consciousness ourselves that we have just not figured out how to tap into it yet.) Most importantly, it seems that all of these special human capabilities emerge out of the self-organizing dynamics of our universe, and in particular the dynamics of the self-organizing, complex adaptive human brain *system* that we are only just beginning to understand.

Given what cosmologists can now observe within our universe and what the rest of us can sense more palpably from within our own solar system, we should not be surprised to find that both the universe and the human brain are fundamentally self-organizing systems. Within both, we can see how different types of "rule-like" behaviors of countless components give rise to a highly decentralized organizing process. Our observable universe appears to consistently organize around the "laws" of thermodynamics, gravity, electromagnetism, and the strong and weak nuclear forces. Our own solar system seems to deploy the "rules" of cellular automata, fractals, autocatalysis, statistical mechanics, genetic algorithms, and Bayesian inference to organize a system wherein order emerges from randomness and chaotic systems. And here on earth, we experience these phenomena in the evolutionary "force" that generates constant innovation and adaptation, replete with recursive, self-referential systems that generate a steady stream of consciousness, creativity, and new ideas. Clearly, the presence of "feedforward" and "feedback" systems is a major aspect of self-organization, as is the form of underlying "intelligence" that gives impetus and sustenance to these processes, even as we struggle to describe the nature of such intelligence or identify its source. Feedforward systems are essential for pushing systems goals and objectives out into operational subsystems, while feedback systems provide the critical information on how well those operational systems are doing in achieving such goals and objectives.

Theologians have their views on its source, but to date cosmologists and physicists have struggled valiantly to define either the source or precise mechanics of such an embedded self-organizing intelligence. To do so, it seems we would need to gain a great deal more purchase on the still hidden mechanics of our universe, and so far nobody can even explain either the origin of the universe or the events leading up to the Big Bang; nobody has deciphered the physics of Dark Energy and Dark Matter, which make up fully 95% of our known universe; and nobody can explain why the "laws" of Nature are as they are, or how the forces of evolution emerged as they did. It seems likely that we may never be able to explain all of these phenomena, and yet our observations of self-organizing dynamics make it clear that some embedded intelligence does exist. It also gives us reason to wonder whether or not the self-organizing nature of the human brain system and the emergent human mind is not in some way both a result and an expression of this higher intelligence. (Eastern philosophy would probably substitute the word "Consciousness" for "intelligence".)

In addition to the elusive nature of this embedded intelligence, there is much that we cannot observe about the self-organizing dynamics of either the universe itself or our own brain systems. We cannot even see the edges of the universe we are confident exist. (The universe has been expanding for almost 14 billion light years, so light from its outer edges would not have had time to reach us yet.) We are still guessing at the self-organizing dynamics that take place between the energy forms, be they "strings" or otherwise, that emerge from, or decay back into, the formless sea of seething energy that some call the "Zero Point Field", "Quantum Vacuum", or "Quantum Loop Gravity". For that matter, we are unable to even observe the self-organizing dynamics of quantum systems, since observation and measurement lead immediately to the collapse of quantum superpositions. The mysteries of phenomena like quantum entanglement persist, and the "uncertainty" that the great physicist Walter Heisenberg taught us was endemic to quantum systems seems to be a fact of life that says a great deal about the world we live in.

So things are uncertain in our universe, which leads our curious minds down the road of endless theorizing, and the theory of self-organization seems like a good place to start. Everything we observe in our little corner of the universe, and about the dynamics of our brain systems, tells us that as random bits of energy and information are converted into ordered ones, systems emerge that reflect a traceable path from limitless possibility to more bounded probability. Everything is dynamic, and there is no certainty. As will be discussed later, it is the nature of our complex adaptive brain systems, and the minds that emerge from them, that they keep searching for "certainty". However, because the fundamental uncertainty embedded in quantum mechanics sits behind all of the laws we observe in our physical surroundings, there simply is no such thing as certainty in our self-organizing world.

The good news is that we can actually measure aspects of that uncertainty and catalogue the statistical mechanics of self-organizing systems. (See Boltzmann Information Theory, below and in Chapter Two.) Moreover, we can analyze with some accuracy how such self-organizing systems grow in complexity, by absorbing, transferring, and generating new information, as they take on increasing levels of organization and higher degrees of probability. In fact, there is perhaps nothing that better defines the nature of our self-organizing universe and human brain systems than their propensity to increase in dynamic complexity, as they generate new component relationships and information.

The presence of dynamic relationships is just one important characteristic of our self-organizing universe. Self-organizing systems are by definition both complex and adaptive, and adaptation requires the presence of both ordered systems and random change. And while self-organizing dynamics provides us with insights into the mechanics of self-assembly, whether in biological or social systems, the dynamics of complex adaptive systems, as discussed in Chapter Five, help us understand why and how systems "learn" and adapt.

To see this, we need look no further than the dynamics of the amazing self-organizing system of evolution. In order to both derive needed solutions to emerging problems and generate new "ideas" that are critical to any self-organizing process, Nature deploys simple genetic algorithms, using recombinant DNA and altering the patterns embedded in genetic Information. There is some element of randomness in the way two sets of parent genes recombine into the chromosomes of offspring, but the randomness that comes from copying errors, genetic mutations, and changes in gene sequencing provides a great deal more leverage to the application of genetic algorithms and the new "ideas" they generate. Random influences, from "noise", error, and other chaotic systems dynamics, are part of the formula that Nature deploys to discard outdated and bad designs, mix in new "ideas", and test the results of those "ideas" to generate better designs. Interestingly, one of the "ideas" that Nature designed early on and that has lasted to this day is the *network* structure of the genome and the processes by which genes are expressed.

This could be a significant factor in how we think about and approach the phenomena of both human intelligence and networked thinking. Biologists and neuroscientists acknowledge that the human body and brain organize themselves partly by genetic design, partly through random processes, and partly from the influences provided by experiential interaction with the environment. In other words, like the universe itself, development of the human brain system seems to involve both the dynamics of network science and some measure of *required* randomness, which is essential to the proper functioning of genetic algorithms. It therefore also seems possible that to optimize the efficiency and intelligence of human thinking, we ought to employ a process that intentionally injects elements of randomness and networked intelligence, as discussed in Chapter Eight and suggested by Figure 2.

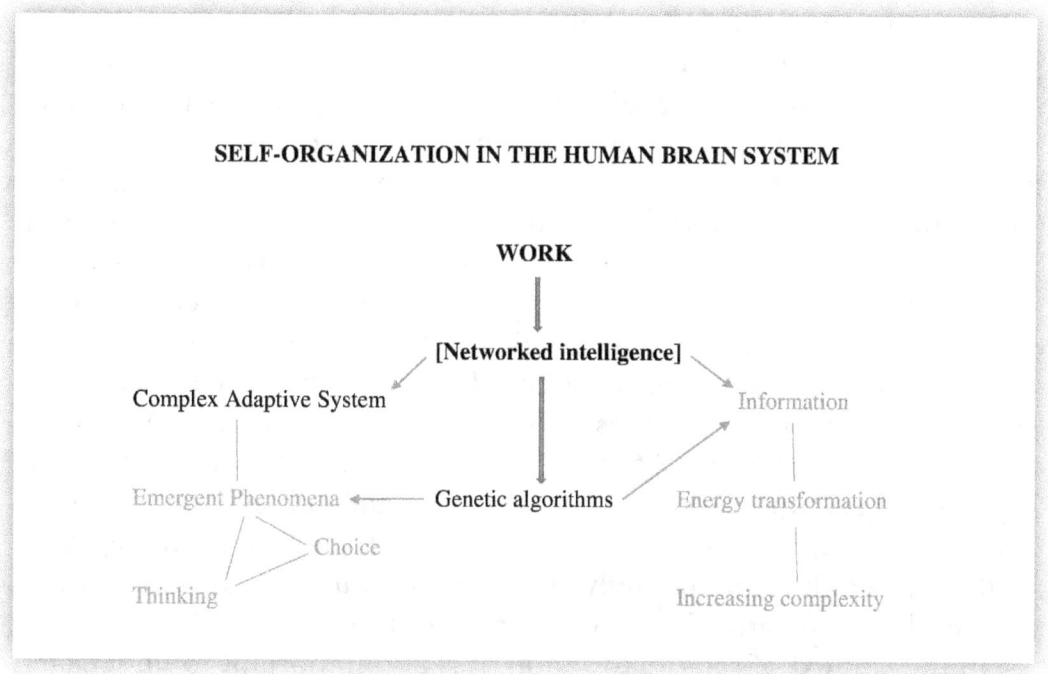

SELF-ORGANIZATION IN THE HUMAN BRAIN SYSTEM

WORK

[Networked intelligence]

Complex Adaptive System   Information

Emergent Phenomena ◄——— Genetic algorithms   Energy transformation

Choice

Thinking   Increasing complexity

Self-organizing, intrinsically "intelligent" systems are decentralized, meaning that there is no central command directing their organizing processes, and for that reason, they must be sustained by various intelligent work processes, which inevitably also inject needed energy and information into the system. Formulaically, perhaps the best way to describe this self-organizing processes would be: $W = TE = I = >C$, in which **W** represents the "Work" that must continue to be injected into such systems to stave off the effects of entropy, **TE** the transformation of energy that takes place when Work is performed, **I** the Information that is transferred to the system, or otherwise manipulated or created in any process of self-assembly, and **>C** the inevitable increase in complexity that naturally results from the universe's embedded self-organizing processes.

Note that the "I" in this formula refers to both "Information" as contemplated by Information Theory and the data or information that we normally think of as the life blood of any complex system. Moreover, this "Information" might be classified as either "Ordered Information", which is generally driven by rules of statistical accumulation and Bayesian updating, or "Random Information", such as the kind Nature uses in its genetic algorithms, mentioned earlier. Viewed in this light, Information provides a useful way to understand the dynamics of change and may even provide a clue on how to manage the challenges most us face in dealing with life's ever increasing complexity.

This formula for self-organization in organic systems is perfectly exemplified by the mechanism through which photons from the sun, of various energy frequencies, manage to inject Work into the most fundamental of chemical systems, transforming the energy configuration of electrons and generating new Information within the system, as it moves into a more complex structure. For example, by altering the electron orbits within specific atoms that make up the molecular structures of carotene and chlorophyll, which are in plentiful supply here on earth, photons of varying frequencies work as "keys" to the applicable atomic "locks", which starts a critical process of organic autocatalysis that is fundamental to self-organizing biological complexity. In the process, these amazing agents of self-organizing biological complexity transfer the "intelligence" of this process into increasingly complex structures as Information that defines the nature and chemical dynamics of those structures.

In the context of self-organization, it is also important to understand how Ludwig Boltzmann's theory of statistical mechanics can be applied to Information Theory in order to explain the relationship between Information and the amount of entropy, or disorganization, within a given system. In the most simple representation, this issue of entropy can be described in the formula: $<I = >P$, or $>I = <P$, which represents the inversely proportional relationship between the amount of Information (I), as defined in Information Theory, in a given system and the Probability (P) of finding that system in a given state. In other words, in a universe that naturally moves toward entropy, the most probable state is a disorganized one, which would be deemed to contain little Information.

Applied to a self-organizing universe, we would say that at the instant of the Big Bang, the universe contained the maximum amount of Information possible, because it existed in the form of a Singularity, which in turn carried all the "instructions" for self-organizing, from the first fraction of a second, going forward to an undefined time span. After that first fraction of a second, as the universe cooled and began to manifest different forms of energy, which ultimately began to organize into systems and manifest as matter, Information flowed into these systems, increasing the Probability of being able to predict and define the organizational dynamics of those systems. This self-organizing principle continues to this day, which is why we say that that quantum systems contain more Information but less predictable organizational states than do physical systems that emerge from the decoherence of such quantum systems. And when it comes to the human brain system, the influence of entropy, and the process of thinking, there is a direct relationship between the degree of order contained in a person's thought and the amount of Information it contains. Fixed, rigid thought processes generate predictable outputs and carry little amounts of Information, while more random and unpredictable processes produce the most creative "ideas" and contain more Information, as defined by Information Theory anyway!

Because of their constant need of energy, Work, and information, self-organizing systems inevitably give rise to self-organizing *information processing and distribution networks*. Information is the life blood of a self-organizing system, especially in terms of how information about system goals and objectives are fed forward into its work processes and how information on the results of those work processes are fed back into the system's adaptive mechanisms. As discussed in Chapter Three, information networks with certain structural characteristics optimize these feedforward and feedback information flows. (Nature favors the use of "Small World" structures, especially in self-organizing biological systems, because they both offer the most cost efficient way to distribute information throughout all the elements of the self-organizing system and remain the most resilient against internal failure or outside attack.)

This is particularly true with respect to the human brain as a self-organizing system. The brain contains hundreds of different cell types, each with its own genetic regulatory, information signaling, and metabolic systems. In one way or another, all these cells are involved in the transfer or creation of information and therefore self-organize into networks, the most important of which are the highly dynamic *neural networks*, which are supported by glial (primarily astrocytes) cell networks. As discussed in Chapter Four, the information processing output of any given neural network in the human brain system is a function of not only which specific neuron or circuits of neurons are connected to each other but which types of neurons or brain cells are involved, what the connection strengths are between and among them, and the timing of their various synaptic connections. The history of synaptic activities among such neurons in the network, as well as the histories of molecular changes within those cells, are two other important factors, as are the many complexities of gene expression and how it drives much of that synaptic activity. Given the complexity of gene-regulation, information-signaling, and metabolic systems dynamics involving all these networks of brain cells, it is not hard to understand why the presence of self-organizing dynamics is so critical to maintaining high level functionality within the human brain system, not to mention a fundamental balance between the influences of ordered and random events.

By their nature, self-organizing systems are difficult to break down and analyze. Self-organizing systems operate in a balance of "circular" cause and effect activities, wherein causes become effects and effects turn into causes, which sometimes makes it very challenging to discern what may be causing the adaptive processes within such systems. Moreover, as detailed in Chapter Five, self-organizing, complex adaptive systems generate all sorts of "emergent phenomena" and "emergent properties", many of which are characterized as "strong", meaning that they can change the structure and dynamics of the very self-organizing systems from which they emerge. The human species' strongly emergent impact on the self-organizing systems of earth's many ecologies, and the human mind's strongly emergent influence on the underlying brain system, are good examples of this reality.

Not surprisingly, the mechanics of networked thinking are highly influenced by the dynamics of self-organizing systems, especially: 1) the complex adaptive dynamics of the human brain system, and the emergent phenomena of human mind and thinking; 2) the self-organizing dynamics within the human brain system surrounding random change and genetic algorithms; 3) the dynamics of self-organizing information networks, and in particular those of a "hierarchical Small World"; 4) how the mechanics of human thinking work with the two major operational human brain systems (Default and Integrated), and the mindsets they generate; 5) how Information self-organizes in human culture; and 6) how human brain systems are networked together in social systems and knowledge bases. All of these factors are discussed in the ensuing chapters of this book.

The Nature of Reality in Our Self-organizing Universe

To fully appreciate the key dynamics of our self-organizing universe, we need to grasp its fundamental structure of "reality". From many different kinds of quantum experiments and cosmological observations, we now know that our universe exists within three basic levels of "reality", though we humans can only physically observe the second and third.

First, there is the "Virtual Reality" that physicists refer to as representing the world we can mathematically approximate but not observe. String theory and M theory have recently attempted to at least define our universe's many dimensions of space, but the conclusions that scientists draw about this level of reality are based on mathematical hypotheses. The human mind finds it difficult to even conceive of space in 10 dimensions, as M theory hypothesizes, so we must rely on esoteric calculus. Virtual reality essentially implies a level of self-organizing in which we may be able to calculate results but have no access to what generates those results, unlike quantum reality, where we have greater understanding of cause and effect.

The quantum level of reality, on the other hand, is where the action is when it comes to information generation and transfer. Here, the randomness and limitless possibility of the virtual world shows evidence of order and measurable probabilities. Here, we begin to find "rules" that govern particle behavior, such as the four nuclear forces—weak, strong, electromagnetic, and gravitational. Here, we can begin to calculate the effect that human agency has in collapsing quantum superpositions, such that mere probability becomes a more predictable reality, one that we can even occasionally apprehend with our five human senses. Here, we are able to observe the effects of the underlying self-organizing intelligence that provides our universe with a perfect balance of order and chaos, one that offers the ideal environment for a self-organizing system like the human brain, whose primary purpose is to predict, observe, learn, and innovate. In fact, there are quite a few physicists, philosophers, and theologians who would assert that the influence human thought can have in defining quantum reality can alter the very direction by which the universe unfolds.

The final level of reality, the material one, is where energy manifests as matter, where quantum possibility and probability are converted into predictable "laws of nature", where chaos generates the "strange attractors" of order, and where self-organizing systems emerge as creative forces. At this level of reality, quantum uncertainty disappears and the influence of quantum mechanics is diminished—here, atoms always combine, under controlled conditions, to form the same molecules, and molecules follow predictable rules in building the materials for all forms of animate and inanimate matter. At this level of reality, we can observe many of the universe's organizing rules and physical phenomena, from fractals and cellular automata to the autocatalytic mechanisms of fundamental biology, all of which contribute to the building of myriad simple and complex systems. (Side note: philosophical speaking, all human reality is to some extent "virtual", as we now know that the "self" we experience in conjunction with our sense of agency in the world is illusory, nothing more than a product of many brain functions that are designed to empower us with feelings of ownership and control over our bodies.)

Understanding how energy and matter manifest within each of these three levels of reality, and the rules and principles that ultimately lead to self-organizing systems dynamics, is vital to tracking the evolution of the human species, our brains, minds, consciousness, and methodologies for thinking. For example, when our social and cultural systems began to self-organize some 50,000 years ago, our brain systems and minds learned how to start making distinctions and compartmentalizing. When we invented written language some 3500 years ago, our brain systems and minds learned how to think sequentially and logically. (As further evidence of the self-organizing nature of culture and of information within human culture, it should be noted that whereas symbols had been used by humans to communicate for some time, there is only one alphabet for all written languages in the West, and it was introduced about 1500 BC.) Simple words, symbolizing things from everyday life, emerged first, but as our human brain systems began to catalogue them as "objects", complex concepts followed quickly, using new vocabularies that allowed our minds to manipulate them in thought, reason, and logic. Thus, it is hardly surprising that the Greek word "logos" has not only been translated into English to mean "word" but provided the foundation for the concept of "logic".

But this is hardly the end of the story about the development of the human brain system and mind. When we discovered quantum mechanics some 100 years ago, our brain systems and minds learned how to embrace the fundamental uncertainty underlying all physical systems and accept the probabilistic nature of our universe. When we discovered the mechanics of DNA and neurophysiology over 50 years ago, our brain systems and minds learned to see new patterns in systems, networks, and various forms of coded information. In the 21st century, our brain systems and minds have evolved to the point that we understand how they self-organize, form dynamic networks, and create moment to moment choices. We understand how a sense of self, intention, and will emerges in the mind, to make choices about how and what we think, even to the point of being able to choose how we might change the structures of our brain systems, the qualities of our consciousness, and the nature of our thoughts.

With this as background, we can begin to appreciate the reasons why the human mind emerges as it does from a vast collection of connected cells, and why the process of human thinking followed on from the systems dynamics of information processing in the brain and the emergent dynamics of mind. Just as the 50 trillion cells of the human body manage to self-organize into a functioning and multi-purposeful whole, so too the 100 billion neurons and 900 billion glial cells in the human brain system manage to self-assemble into hundreds of functional networks, systems, and emergent capabilities. No principles of genetic coding, gene expression, or even epigenetics can explain how a system of over 50 trillion cells, each one processing information and generating tens of thousands of chemical events every second, can synchronize and organize themselves in such a way as to give rise to a sentient, self-aware, highly intelligent being. Self-organizing systems are mysteriously intelligent, pure and simple, so we should not be surprised to find that phenomena as amazing as the human mind and thought might also emerge from a process of self-organization.

Finally, it should be noted that we have begun to contemplate how our brains might have quantum computational capabilities, which could even allow us to generate thoughts and other mental capacities that draw upon information that is captured holographically within the universe. Granted, we are a long way from either being able to confirm such capabilities or describe their physical mechanics, but this is the type of emergent knowledge that continues to provide us insight into who we are and how our brain systems generate the phenomenon of self-awareness, which lies at the root of our unique intelligence. Just as we can never hope to observe and explain everything that goes on at the virtual level of reality in our known universe, there may be aspects of quantum reality that forever remain elusive and incapable of modeling, but it behooves us now to at least consider all the possibilities. We are, after all, apparently growing increasingly self-aware and self-conscious. More so than at any other time in human history, we now have the tools to gain critical insights into the dynamics of our self-organizing brain systems and the thought processes that emerge from them; we can begin to appreciate the true nature of the choices that come before us.

Toward that end, the next two chapters will address the mechanics and dynamics of Information Theory and networks, which are essential aspects of our self-organizing universe and critical to our understanding of the human brain system and how it generates networked thinking.

2

INFORMATION THEORY

Information Theory, as originally conceived by Claude Shannon back in the mid-20th century, revolved around a few distinctive concepts: identifiable bits (1's and 0's) of data, or Information (referred to as Shannon Information, or just Information, with a capital "I"), a defined message, and the "noise" surrounding that message. Shannon, a Bell Labs mathematician and engineer, was primarily concerned with the challenge of how much messages sent along phone lines could be compressed without losing their integrity.

Applied to the concept of self-organizing systems, Shannon's Information Theory carries two major implications. The first involves any situation in which a specific outcome or answer can be characterized in a string of bits, as is the case in all computer programming. In this case, the amount of Information contained in the answer is the minimum number of bits necessary to transmit the answer message from sender to receiver. For example, in self-organizing systems, this might be the information contained in a message that is delivered through one of its critical feedback systems.

The second important aspect of Information Theory applied to self-organizing systems is more relevant to the open-ended dynamics of such systems and how they are always evolving and becoming more complex. In this case, the best way to describe Shannon's theory would be to say that Information is directly proportional to the *improbability* of its content. So we would conclude in this context that the orderly formation of our universe, galaxy, solar system, planet earth, and human species that has occurred over the last 13.7 billion year is almost incalculably improbable, which means that there is a tremendous amount of Information embedded in it. (Physicist Fred Hoyle once estimated that the odds of our universe and solar system coming together as they did, with conditions that support life as we know it on earth, are somewhere in the neighborhood of 1 in 10 to the 100th power.)

In similar fashion, the improbabilities of how the human brain system emerged as it did from long-standing evolutionary processes, ultimately giving rise to the emergence of a mind such as ours, are staggeringly large. When we contemplate how each human brain system self-organizes itself into endless numbers of unique configurations, generating separate and distinct minds, personalities, and the like, the improbabilities of the world we live in become even more amazing. Thus, according to Information Theory, there is a tremendous amount of Information stored within each self-organizing human brain/mind, separate and distinct from the Information that is processed and computed within each one of them, every second.

To further emphasize this point in a very practical example, we would say that it is highly improbable that letters would arrange themselves into a particular message, so when such a message emerges, it contains a certain amount of Information related to the way in which the message is formed. In this way, Information Theory explains the self-organizing process of written languages, where letters combine together in certain identifiable order and patterns to form words, and words recur in similar types of patterns to form sentences. Viewed from this perspective, it seems that there must be a deep and important correlation between the amount of Information contained in self-organizing systems and the presence of the underlying "intelligence" that appears to drive the mechanics of self-assembly.

From these two perspectives, we are able to see how Information reduces uncertainty and is therefore related to the concept of Work in self-organizing systems. As we will see in later chapters, this insight is critical to our understanding of the self-organizing system that is the human brain, as well as to the many processes of Information processing and communication that are undertaken within the human brain/mind. Whether it involves phone lines, fiber optic cables, or the human brain system, processing and transmitting messages are "expensive" undertakings—major consumers of energy in the brain, or bandwidth in communication networks. For example, certain visual processing systems of the human brain have to encode pieces of visual data and forward them for integration and interpretation in other parts of the brain, but the data (Information bits) that arrive do not form a complete, redundant image. Instead, Information stored in memory accumulates enough certainty from the available data to create a meaningful visual image, essentially "filling in the blanks" to create the "picture" that emerges in our mind's eye. (Neuroscientists have also recently discovered a parallel process in the somatosensory regions of the brain that manage the dynamics of touch.)

None of this is terribly surprising, as the human brain could not possibly afford to process and transmit every last bit of sensory stimuli with optimal redundancy, because doing so would consume too much time and energy. Much the same is true in social or family systems and the conventions we use to communicate messages in our daily lives. You could not afford to spell out every last suggestion, thought, idea, instruction, or the like in your communication with family members, friends, and work colleagues, or you would never be able to accomplish all the things that need to be done to survive and thrive. Of course, this can lead to serious cases of miscommunication too, but it simply reflects the reality of a universe filled with Information, where the effectiveness of message transfer must be balanced against the costs of doing so, where certainty may sometimes be critical but redundancy is often a luxury.

As an aside, Shannon's theory was not directed at "Quantum Information", which, because of its inherently uncertain nature, likely manifests as superpositions of probabilities that only take on characteristics of Shannon Information following quantum collapse. Nevertheless, there are some who are now seeking to apply Information Theory to quantum systems.

Shannon's theory also suggests that Information can be embedded in a system to help supply the level of certainty required to interpret a message or pattern of data. Such embedded Information might appear to be some form of "intelligence", as perhaps in the case of self-organizing systems, or simply different forms of procedural and semantic knowledge. For example, to even start trying to crack the code of the famous World War II German Enigma Machine, Allan Turning and his Bletchley Park gang (recently brought to light on the silver screen in *The Imitation Game*) first had to figure out how the machine worked mechanically. Once they solved that, they could try to find the elements of redundancy in the coded messages that leaked some key bits of Information, which could then be compared to other messages and leveraged to decipher subsequent messages. Once they had that Information, they gained the "intelligence" to decipher the Enigma Machine's code.

Perhaps another example of a simple, more common application of Information Theory would also be useful. A message that is certain to be fully and accurately transmitted, such as a text that says

"Meet you at 6PM, in front of the Waldorf Hotel", contains high levels of certainty, and redundancy. On the other hand, assuming the receiver has the requisite Information or "intelligence", a text that says "Mt @ 6, W hotel" retains the essential Information to communicate the desired message, using less bits, making it faster for the sender to send (theoretically saving valuable brain energy and personal time) as well as cheaper for the wireless carrier to transmit. For example, suppose the sender and receiver had had an earlier conversation in which the sender suggested a meeting at either the Waldorf or the nearby Yale Club, to which his companion (the subsequent message receiver) had simply replied "You decide the time and place, then send me a text." Assuming no one else was around to hear the conversation, the sender and receiver would be the only two people in the world who would have the "intelligence" to be *certain* about the intended message of the subsequent text. This concept of Information as embedded intelligence leads to one of the main reasons that networked thinking and Knowledge Networks are able to generate important new forms of intelligence, as discussed in Chapters Eight and Nine.

While Shannon was primarily interested in figuring out the most cost effective way configure or compress messages across telephone lines, he gave birth to a very important (and still somewhat emergent) science. During the latter half of the 20th century, physicists began to form their own versions of Information Theory, based on Shannon's principles, which they applied to help explain some of the important enigmas embedded in the laws of thermodynamics and complexity science. Today, when a physicist applies the principles of Information Theory, he or she refers to a much broader concept than Shannon's, wherein all manifested energy within the universe is said to contain, and essentially be defined by, its own unique Information set. From the wave functions of a quantum particle or system to the nature of a quark's spin, the electron orbit of a hydrogen atom, and so forth, Information defines every particular manifestation of energy and matter, as well as the interrelationships that created those energy or matter forms in the first place. For this reason, physicists would say that at the precise moment of the Big Bang, the singularity that was to become our expanding universe contained all the Information that exists within the universe today.

Physics in the 21st century has essentially become the study of probabilities, with quantum mechanics being the most uncertain, "noisy", and wide-ranging probabilistic systems, which therefore contain considerable Information, and Newtonian physical systems, which operate within an ambit of predictable mechanics and therefore contain less Information. While quantum systems are held in superposition, their Information is uncertain and hard to access, subject to variable interactions with other quantum and non-quantum systems, so wave functions are reflected in probability profiles of how they may interact with other systems. Once those quantum systems collapse into manifestations of energy and structures that can be observed and analyzed, using the laws of Nature, it is much easier to predict how they will interact with other physical systems. All of which suggests that quantum systems contain not only considerable Information but untapped intelligence as well, even though their unpredictability makes it difficult to access such hidden intelligence. In Chapter Eight, we will see how this set of dynamics parallels the emergence of increasingly unpredictable but powerful organizational levels of mind and thought.

For purposes of this book on networked thinking, it is important to understand both the simple mechanics of Shannon Information Theory and the more elusive principles of Information Theory applied to the laws of physics. This is particularly true with respect to Information that defines the *relationship between* elements of a complex system, be they the smallest quanta of energy in a quantum system or the "objects" that the human brain system uses to catalogue everything it encounters and needs to manipulate in order to survive. Why? Because the human brain system basically relies on Information Theory dynamics to help it gauge the probabilities embedded in the relationships between things, especially the components of complex systems. For example, the human brain system makes associations between "objects" by identifying the information patterns they have in common and discarding the information it deems irrelevant ("noise" in Information Theory).

Essentially, we have the work of Ludwig Boltzmann in statistical mechanics to thank for this insight. Boltzmann was a physicist who predated Shannon's work by 50 years, but by applying his principles of statistical mechanics to Information Theory, mathematicians, physicists, chemical engineers, and even network scientists have been able to better understand and explain 1) the fundamental balance in Nature between chaos and order, 2) the dynamics of complex systems and the effect of entropy on them, and 3) how to define the various manifestations of Work that allow such systems to (at least temporarily) forestall the disordering effects of entropy. "Boltzmann Information Theory" uses probability theory to define the relationship between Information and levels of entropy, or disorder, in systems. So, Boltzmann Information Theory would say that the higher the probability of a given distribution within a closed system, the more entropy (and the less Information) it contains. For example, if you toss a box full of marbles down on the floor, the most probable result will be a random, highly entropic, distribution of all different shapes and colors. But if you then go to the effort of sorting them all into groups of similar shapes and colors, you will have provided the Work necessary to reduce the randomness of their distribution. The most probable state for the marbles when you released them was a disorganized one (high entropy), but once you added the Work of sorting those marbles, you reduced the entropy and added Information to the "system".

These key aspects of Information Theory are particularly relevant to networked thinking, for two reasons. First, Information Theory suggests that if the human brain system processes all kinds of different Information bits, within different types of networks and systems, outputs in the form of behaviors and thoughts will manifest along a range of probability profiles, in terms of how much order and clarity of message they reflect. As will be discussed in Chapter Seven, the human brain system operates largely on two different scales, depending on whether its Default or Integrated system is in control. Accordingly, it may be possible to adjust our behaviors and thinking toward various levels of desired order and message clarity, depending on how Information is processed within the Default and Integrated systems.

Second, Information Theory helps us understand one of the subtle but significant processes involved in networked thinking—synthesis. As noted in Chapter Seven, the Integrated brain system uses many different feedforward and feedback systems to deliver various forms of synthesis, and when it synthesizes sets of Information and knowledge into patterns of increasing simplicity, it enhances probabilities that the intended messages will be clearly transmitted throughout the system's networks. Recent research indicates that as relevant Information and knowledge are processed in the human brain system, the neural networks involved in such processing initially expand but shortly thereafter contract, suggesting that synthesis makes such networks increasingly cohesive and efficient. Information Theory tells us that higher levels of message clarity and order within such networks means that the larger system has absorbed Information, probably in the form of processing efficiency and synthesized Information patterns.

When it comes to the laws of thermodynamics, physicists treat Information more like energy, which cannot be created or destroyed, only transformed.

Accordingly, it is often useful to refer to either "Random" or "Ordered" Information, in the context of how Information from chaotic systems becomes ordered in complex adaptive systems. Both this approach to Information and the concept generated by Shannon Information Theory should therefore be distinguished from the way that the information is thought of by complexity scientists, or the way we use the word "information" colloquially, with a small "i". In complexity science, the concept of "information" can carry either the colloquial meaning or that employed by Information Theory. In complex systems, information represents a dynamic concept, emerging from the processing of data and the interaction of elements within the system, so complexity scientists think of information as something both that is both processed and created by them. So while physicists might say that, like energy, Information cannot be created or destroyed, complexity scientists would treat information as something that is constantly being processed, manipulated, transformed, created, and destroyed.

The Dynamics of Information Theory Applied to Networks in Complex Adaptive Systems

As will be discussed in the next chapter, most self-organizing networks whose primary role is to efficiently distribute Information are made up of numerous "hubs", giving rise to a "Small World" structure. There is always a "cost" associated with the distribution of information within any system, and Small World networks are highly cost efficient, meaning that they effectively identify information that is highly salient to the operational processes of the system in which they are embedded, before proceeding to the "costly" distribution of such information throughout the system. Information Theory dynamics play an important role in this process in two distinct ways. First, the very process by which the human brain system determines the relevance and salience of information flowing in from outside the system is influenced by the way such information is stylized, or encoded in messages. Information that is too "cryptic" for the human brain system to recognize gets ignored, but so do messages and information packets that are too redundant, large, and cumbersome to process within brain system processing time frames (generally in the hundreds of milliseconds). Information that the human brain system might have considered relevant and salient may not make the cut because of how much or little Shannon Information it contains. Sometimes this means the Information is not processed at all.

Other times, it means that the information cannot be processed in Working Memory and is therefore not attended to in the conscious mind, as discussed in Chapters Four and Six.

Second, given its goal of cost efficiently distributing such relevant and salient information throughout its entire information processing network, the human brain system must itself employ the space/energy saving techniques of Information Theory in facilitating information distribution. No system is perfect, and in any information distribution process messages will be inadvertently corrupted or mistakenly transmitted. It is simply a reality to be mindful of, particularly when it comes to the conscious, strategic, and directed practice of networked thinking. Anyone who has played the childhood game of "Telephone" knows how distorted messages can become within any given human mind, and even more so when transferred between such minds!

In summary, Information Theory explains how messages are most efficiently formulated and transmitted, which has direct application to the way the human brain processes Information and internally signals its messages; it helps explain the mechanism behind the self-organizing dynamics of systems like the complex adaptive human brain; it describes the nature of the Work that is required to organize a system and prevent it from falling back into disorder, as the 2nd Law of Thermodynamics states that it should; and it helps explain how and why messages and other Information sets are most effectively transmitted through networks.

As discussed in Chapter Seven, Shannon Information Theory also offers useful insight into the way our human brain systems "chunk" bits of Information and manipulate them into patterns to form critical messages of all kinds, which are transmitted throughout the brain and the rest of the body. These Information patterns give rise to the "objects" the human brain's Default system creates to help our minds visualize and navigate both the tangible and intangible world around us.

The Dynamics of How Information Self-organizes in Human Culture

The Small World structure of the human brain system's information processing and distribution networks has another very significant ramification, related to how Information self-organizes in human culture. Like so many other systems in our solar system, human social and cultural systems are self-organizing, and they do so for reasons ranging from the need for social order to the desire to share diverse facets of human creative expression. In the case of culture, the dynamics of self-organization seek to balance the randomness that is generated by individual freedom of expression and self-interest on the one hand with the order that is necessary to promote widespread collaboration and collective intelligence on the other. Within this self-organizing balance, a whole raft of human behaviors reflect the various felt and perceived needs we have to survive, procreate, recreate, express our creative thoughts and feelings, belong in community, share ideas, and what not. And because all of these human behaviors are defined, like everything else in our universe, by the Information they contain, it quickly becomes quite evident how Information self-organizes in human culture.

For example, clearly there is Information that self-organizes in human culture around basic human survival needs and the fundamental demands of the human brain. In today's industrialized world, very few people grow their own food, so knowledge and processes have emerged over time around the need to harvest, preserve, store, label, and transport food. What are all the modern inventions of farming equipment, food preservation, and packaging if not self-organizing units of Information that define new products, services, and processes? What are grocery stores compared to roadside food stands if not simply assemblies of Information and knowledge that have self-organized into increasingly more complex structures, based on the fundamental human need to eat, especially when there are many of us gathered in dense urban areas?

And in like fashion, one could say that fast-food chains are just a particular Information pattern that self-organized around the perceived needs of modern humans to eat and save time. Likewise, markets, communication systems, and transportation technologies all self-organize to some extent around human needs. Moving on from basic needs to activities of procreation, recreation, and creative expression, are not the concepts of marriage, all the various types of sporting activities, and creative arts ranging from painting to symphonies merely self-organizing units of Information in human culture? The list goes on and on.

We should not be surprised by either the self-organization of Information in culture or its similarity to the self-organizing dynamics of information in evolutionary processes, as they basically involve similar sets of dynamics. Interestingly, a few decades ago, evolutionary biologist Richard Dawkins looked at what I see as units of self-organizing Information in culture and coined them "memes", so as to suggest how similar their copying and spreading processes were to those of genes. According to Dawkins and others like Susan Blakemore, a meme can be thought is a unit of culture that can be copied, varied, selected for, and retained, in a somewhat parallel fashion to the way information in genes is passed on through natural selection. In both cases, there is deep historicity, learning, and evolutionary dynamics involved. Here is the key distinction though—memes can only be passed on by and through imitation of other human behavior, just as information coded in genes is passed on only through DNA. So just as genes carry instructions for the creation of proteins, turning on of other genes, and so forth, memes must contain the instructions for copying the behavior associated with the content of the meme. Using this definition, it is clear that private thoughts and feelings would not be memes, because they cannot be imitated, but virtually everything else I have mentioned would qualify.

Not coincidentally, humans are the greatest imitators in the world, and we have developed the most extensive set of copying tools, such as written languages, video recording, even the cameras we conveniently carry around with us in our mobile phones. So for example, a carrot cake is a meme, and it can be copied, varied, and selected for in any number of forms by 1) watching another person make one, 2) reading a recipe, 3) listening to your mother tell you how to make one, 4) watching a video of Julia Childs making one, etc. According to the theory of memetics, the more fidelity a meme carries, and the more fertile an environment is for the copying of that meme, the more likely it is to be selected for and retained for a long time.

Because of the way they are copied, varied, and selected for in individual and collective human brains, memes are effectively another way of describing units of self-organizing information in human culture, even though Dawkins' approach does not use the same terminology or methodology for perpetuation. In any event, for the sake of convenience, I will refer to self-organizing Information in culture throughout the rest of this book as "memes", and I will also use Dawkins' construct for meme replication and selection.

It would be hard to overemphasize the importance of memes when it comes to human thought processes. As explained in Chapter Four, most of the Information that bombards our brain systems every day is processed outside our awareness, but not beyond the reach of our memory systems. We are superb imitators, and many of the behaviors and thoughts we *consciously* think are original to our own brain systems and minds are in fact nothing more than memes that have become embedded in our minds without our even realizing it.

Like genes, memes are not inherently "good" or "bad"—they simply self-organize and spread. And just as genes require organisms in which to be copied, varied, selected for, and passed on to future generations, so memes require the human brain/mind to do the same. Consciously or not, we humans are carriers of Information that has self-organized into patterns that eventually become concepts and ideas, all of which directly affect our thoughts and behaviors. That said, there is much to be gained from memes, provided we are mindful of their existence and careful about which ones we allow to fill our minds and thoughts. For the most part, memes represent vital pieces of learning and synthesis that others have created for us and that we merely need to copy—or vary in some way to suit our own personal needs—in order to benefit from centuries of experimentation and learning by many of our ancestors. Just think of the history of a simple meme like a knife, conceived of long ago by ancestors who had to cut up their prey and share it within their clans, but which has been copied and varied so many times and ways over the years that today we use high powered blenders to do our sophisticated food processing.

Of course, even though memes are not themselves "bad" we should also be wary of the memes that have potential counterproductive *consequences* attached to them, such as memes dealing with violent behaviors and the memes that help spread them, like some video games. But for the most part, memes are simply what happens when Information self-organizes around human physical and cultural needs, and it is what we do with such memes that matters most. The important point here is that we need to be mindful that memes exist and how much they invade our thoughts, especially unconsciously.

Accordingly, memes need to be factored into the dynamics of networked thinking. Some memes may be copied and varied in a whole host of human brain systems and minds in such a way as to simplify their instructions for imitating certain human behavior, thereby enhancing their ability to be selected and spread. For example, memes related to communication protocols moved very quickly from "snail mail" to email to texting, because the form of the communication made imitation increasingly easier at each step. (Not more eloquent, but easier!) But guess what—as each of these newly varied memes was selected for by major segments of the population, it gave rise to communications that became increasingly unpredictable, semantically cryptic, and "noisy" as well. Remember, because the Information in them has become increasingly compressed, the messages in texts can be more ambiguous and uncertain than those in emails and letters, which subjects them to higher probabilities of misinterpretation. As discussed further in Chapter Eight, networked thinking takes these dynamics into account. Parenthetically, and to underscore the dynamics of why and how Information self-organizes in cultural as well as in physical systems, note how snail mail letters emerged from the basic need of humans to communicate, then quickly varied into the email and texting memes because of the ever-increasing *perceived* need for speed in our current world!

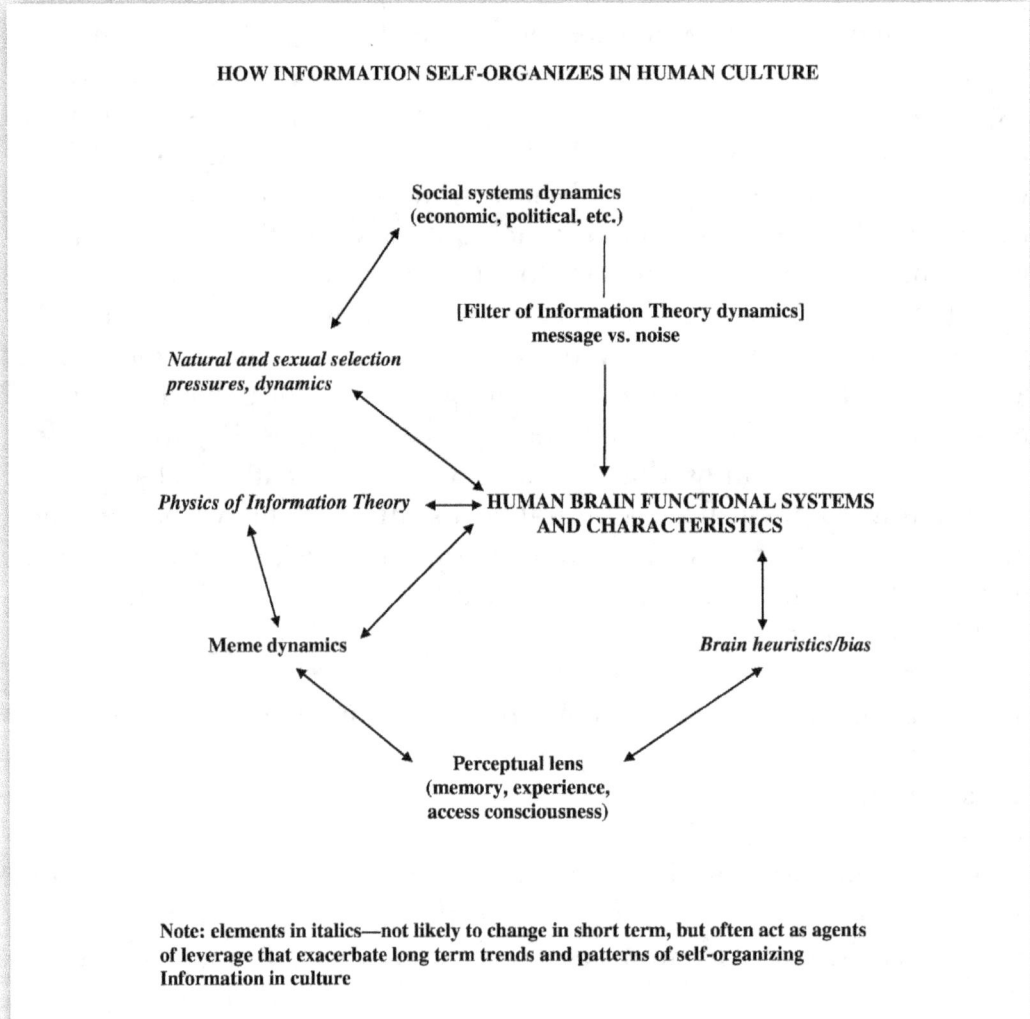

HOW INFORMATION SELF-ORGANIZES IN HUMAN CULTURE

Social systems dynamics
(economic, political, etc.)

[Filter of Information Theory dynamics]
message vs. noise

*Natural and sexual selection
pressures, dynamics*

Physics of Information Theory ←→ HUMAN BRAIN FUNCTIONAL SYSTEMS
AND CHARACTERISTICS

Meme dynamics

Brain heuristics/bias

Perceptual lens
(memory, experience,
access consciousness)

Note: elements in italics—not likely to change in short term, but often act as agents of leverage that exacerbate long term trends and patterns of self-organizing Information in culture

3

THE DYNAMICS OF NETWORKS

From the point of view of cosmology and physics, the two scientific disciplines that seek to explain the general mechanics of our known universe, everything that goes on ultimately revolves around the phenomenon of Information, particularly how it is created, processed, and shared. While the last chapter dealt with what Information is and how it is created, this one focuses primarily on how it is shared, particularly through networks.

As detailed in Chapter Five, complex adaptive systems form around specific goals and teleology, relying on internal rules and adaptive intelligence to keep "learning" and updating their operational strategies, based on the flow of information that is constantly being fed forward and fed back through the systems in question. Networks, on the other hand, self-organize, both inside and outside Nature, into different kinds of structures, depending on what types of information they are transferring, the information flow requirements of a particular system, the risk of network failure, and how critical such failure would be to the operational dynamics of the system. Given these parameters, we might expect that the complex adaptive human brain system has many different types of neural networks but one overarching, dominant structure.

So networks are designed to exchange information, and as it relates to the whole subject of networked thinking, it is important to note that complex adaptive systems like the human brain rely on two basic kinds of information: 1) organizing information (and order-generating energy), which is necessary to stave off the forces of entropy, and 2) randomized information, which is necessary to generate new ideas and adaptive responses. Both the human brain system and the larger system of the whole body contain millions of networks that are structured to strike the perfect balance between efficient distribution and tolerance of extraordinary stresses. As will be discussed in more detail later, this particular network structure, referred to as "Small World", naturally self-organizes within virtually all organic complex adaptive systems, and quite a few inorganic ones as well. This latter category includes both physical ones (electrical grids, highway and airline networks, the Internet) and intangible ones (social and professional networks, the World Wide Web, economies).

Network dynamics derive from three primary factors: *structure, information flow mechanics, and environmental context.* In the case of personal networks, there is a fourth factor, where human agency adds a set of interpersonal dynamics.

- Structural dynamics of networks revolve around the way nodes "cluster"—in other words, where a few nodes are heavily linked to each other in a close network and also have lots of links (or "ties") to other nodes, such that there is a short link path between any two nodes. As discussed further below, the links between nodes in a network can be either "weak" or "strong", "directed" or "undirected". So the links within a cluster are "strong" and may be "directed" (information flowing in one direction) or "undirected" (information flowing in both directions). Links to the nodes outside the cluster are considered "weak" and also can be either directed or undirected. As nodes and links are added to random networks, they tend to become more ordered, and as they are added to ordered networks, they tend to form into certain types of "Small World" and "Scale Free" configurations.
- Information flow mechanics deals with the type of information that is being transferred within the network, how the information is transmitted and received, and various other issues related to Information Theory.
- Environmental context involves the interrelationship dynamics between a particular network and the environment in which it operates, such as how neural networks in the human brain are formulated and reformulated based on the sensory information that is being continually processed within the brain system or the changes that are constantly occurring in the body's biochemistry and the brain's neurotransmitter levels.

Network Structure

Structural elements that affect network dynamics include not just levels of order or randomness but how nodes are connected to each other, creating patterns of "degree distance" that technically determines how far any given node is from another. Adding strong ties to random networks and weak ties to ordered networks tends to enhance their cohesiveness and provide them with greater information transfer efficiency.

For purposes of this book on networked thinking, four network structures are particularly relevant: Random, Ordered, Small World, and Scale Free. Each has a vital information processing and distribution role within self-organizing systems:

1. Random networks deliver valuable new bits of information that are vital to the execution of genetic algorithms and adaptive change within such systems;

2. Ordered networks are the most stable networks and potentially the fastest at distributing information within certain sub-networks (especially clusters) but not the most effective in feeding information forward and back throughout the entire network;

3. Small World networks offer the optimal combination of stability and efficiency of information processing/distribution throughout the whole network and is therefore the most common type in self-organizing and other complex adaptive systems, where the need for efficient information transfer is so high; and

4. Scale Free networks, which result from particular systems dynamics that generate an emergent phenomenon of "preferential attachment" and grow exponentially bigger, according to the mathematics of "power laws"; they can be effective at synthesizing information but threaten the even flow of information throughout the network and are more vulnerable to internal failure and external attack than Small World ones.

As stated earlier, undirected links generate two way information exchange, whereas directed ones tend to send information in one direction only, and usually for a "directed" purpose. A commanding Army officer's order usually establishes directed links with the soldiers in his platoon, though sometimes feedback is called for on how successfully the order was carried out, or not. (And to add the Information Theory context, these orders are also certain and redundant, devoid of much "noise".) Clearly, the operating and information exchange dynamics of a network will differ greatly, depending on whether the majority of its links are undirected or directed. For example, in a small professional network where most of the links will likely be undirected, the type of information exchanged within the network, the velocity of information flow, the degrees of reciprocity in such exchanges, and even the handling of the exchanged information may vary widely, depending on the nature of the interpersonal relationships behind those professional links. A veteran neurosurgeon in a ten person physician network might completely ignore an email sent by a newly-minted vascular surgeon on a new development in interventional radiology, but the same neurosurgeon will likely get detailed responses from all the nurses in his practice from whom he has requested a specific type of patient information.

Network Structural Dynamics

Given that they exist to distribute information, networks are basically products of the interplay between order and chaos, structure and environment, design and randomness. The famous mathematician Paul Erdos was an early pioneer of network science and a major contributor to our understanding of how various network structures emerge as a result of these interplays. Working initially with random networks, Erdos discovered that only a small percentage of all the possible links between points on a graph would be required to create a network that connected every point. For example, a graph of 300 points and 50,000 possible links only required 2 % of randomly placed links to connect all the points into a virtual network.

It is all well and good that it does not take a great number of links to connect disparate nodes to form a network, since creating network links generally incurs a "cost" of some sort (e.g., laying down fiber optic cables in a LAN), but laying down the links is only half the battle. Though Erdos' finding means networks can be built at very low cost, the actual flow of information within such random networks will be difficult to monitor and control. Highly ordered networks, on the other hand, carry a high degree of certainty and redundancy in terms of information transfer but are expensive to set up and operate, as they necessarily have a great number of links that connect each node to every other node in the network. The human brain, for example, could never be designed as a highly ordered network, given its size constraints and the amount of energy that would be required to operate that type of network. (As noted in the next chapter, the human brain system uses various shortcuts and extrapolations to make up for the lack of redundancy in its information processing networks and systems.)

Enter Mark Granovetter. A network science pioneer in the 1970s, Granovetter noted that certain networks, like social ones, are defined by the nature of their "ties" and that the "strong" ties between people tended to create triangles, which in turn were connected to each other in small groups by additional strong ties or more randomly connected to more remote triangular networks via "weak" ties. More importantly, for purposes of delving into the specifics of network thinking, Granovetter showed that removing one link from such hypothetical triangles did not have a significant impact on the "social connectivity" of any one person, and it was the nature and number of weak ties that determined how effective a social network might be in exchanging information. (For this reason, anyone who is networking in pursuit of a job should spend more time with his or her weak-tie contacts within a social or professional network, as mere acquaintances (weak ties) are much more effective than close friends (strong ties) at widely distributing a resume or hearing about a broad range of opportunities.)

This is a very subtle but important aspect of network mechanics, especially as it relates to the concept of Knowledge Networks discussed in Chapter Nine. It may be true that eliminating one of the strong ties that holds together a given triangular communication sub-network does not significantly impact the overall connectivity of the network at large, but it does affect the efficiency and integrity of the information flow within that triangle. For example, if I represented one node (C) in that hypothetical triangle, and I counted on each of the other two nodes, A and B, to supply me with two distinct sets of critical information, I would really need to be connected to each separately to insure that I receive the necessary information, in a *timely* manner and unadulterated by the nature of the relationship and communication styles between A and B.

In similar fashion, in an information processing network like the human brain system, if information from any of the neural networks/circuits/systems in a triangular network—let's call them A (dealing with memory recall) and B (processing of an emotion)—is not fed directly into network/circuit/system C, at just the right time, the resulting decision, behavior, thought, feeling, etc. produced in the brain/mind will certainly be different than if a direct information feed had occurred. Strong, undirected triangular networks with nodes that easily and efficiently exchange information, generate feedback, and even synthesize some of that information to make it more valuable to every node in the network, are essential to the proper functioning of the human brain system. (Everyone is familiar with this phenomenon of "broken links" in the brain, or perhaps more likely just delayed performance in the links, because all of us have struggled from time to time to come up with a word, name, or thought that we know we know and which seems to sit right on the "tip of my tongue".)

In the late 20th century, two other mathematicians, Duncan Watts and Steven Strogarz, made another set of interesting discoveries. Using sophisticated computer modeling, they proved that by randomly adding more and more links to a random network, clusters began to form, which decreased the "degree distribution" of the network, making it more cohesive. In today's popular networking world, this would be known as reducing the "degrees of separation" between two people who do not know each other directly. Moreover, using the same computer modeling techniques, Watts and Strogarz also discovered that when random links were added to a highly ordered network made up of small clusters, the network's degree distribution also dropped significantly, which eventually helped them realize the overall benefits created by self-organizing networks comprised of multiple clusters, connected by strategically placed weak ties.

Thanks to Granovetter's work, they knew that in social networks clusters would be made up of many different triangular sub-networks, but Watts and Strogarz later determined that how clusters formed varied greatly, depending on the type of information flowing through them and how that information was being used. For example, molecular networks in cells, which use a limited number of gene and protein networks and exchange information between molecules very rapidly, form a few highly concentrated clusters that serve as communication "hubs". Neural networks in the human brain, on the other hand, are less "centralized" than molecular networks, with numerous and widely distributed clusters that are highly interconnected, so that information can be discretely processed for specific purposes before being more widely shared within the network. For example, once emotion is processed in the limbic system, information representing that emotional content is sent to many other functional systems across the brain, from the cerebellum to sensorimotor cortical systems and the many cognitive systems in the neo-cortex.

Ultimately, Watts and Strogartz discovered that most networks found in Nature, and a good many other (inorganic) real world networks as well, self-organize into clusters that connect up, using the benefit of weak ties, to form what they termed "Small World" networks. (In the Network Science terminology used by Strogarz and Watts, Small World networks have high "clustering coefficients" and low "degree distributions".) Small World networks prove to be Nature's choice time and time again, particularly because their flexible structures make it easy for them to adapt to uneven information flows and changes in their environments.

Small World networks tend to have large numbers of similarly sized clusters that are connected to each other and to other nodes through weak ties, which makes distribution of information within the network quick and efficient. Within such a structure, it is easy to design "self-similarity", building the same kind of triangles, pentagons, or other forms of clusters that are endemic to self-organizing systems and their orientation toward efficiency. The "self- similarity" embedded in fractal structures, whether found in river beds, tree structures, or snowflakes, serves the same type of "purpose" in Nature that Small World networks do, building in capacity and tolerance of failure as the volume of information (or water, in the case of river fractals!) demands. With many similarly sized and widely dispersed clusters, Small World networks can survive both internal random node or link failure and random attacks on nodes or links from exogenous sources.

Moreover, because information is easily exchanged among nodes in the clusters of Small World networks, their structures optimize the two way (undirected) flow of information, which generates important feedback and maximizes the opportunity for synthesis and learning from such feedback. The complex adaptive human brain system is itself a hierarchically structured set of Small World networks, and neuroscientists have recently begun to focus on the information processing implications of synaptic firing "synchrony" within the brain system's neural networks. It is quite possible that only Small World network structures could give rise to the type of electromagnetic wave synchrony that has been observed to emerge across the entire brain system, at 40Hz, which has been tied to various mental phenomena, such as certain aspects of consciousness.

Though Small World networks have interesting structural dynamics ramifications in inorganic networks as well, this is a book about how the most complex organic network—in the human brain system—processes information and ultimately engages in "thinking", so I will continue to focus in this chapter on the network science embedded in Nature. In order to keep innovating and evolving, Nature constantly generates new "ideas" and tests them for "fitness", subjecting them to "competitive pressures", and selecting the "winners". This process relies on the stable exchange of information within genetic networks and the millions of "experimental trials" generated by Nature's genetic algorithms, which take place in the proving ground of competitive pressures that emerge from within a given environment. To do this, Nature needs to take the occasional risk. That "risk" has been known to biologists for years—mutation in genes and their complicated sequencing can produce all sorts of damage and disease, even threatening the survival of entire species. But in a universe that exists within an ongoing tension of chaos and order, there is only one rule that applies to all of Nature's systems—no risk, no creative growth. We humans have minds that are capable of doing amazing things, including complex thinking, thanks to the risk that Nature has taken over millions of years in the networking of genome sequences and Promoter genes.

In conjunction with that risk, Nature sometimes favors a shift from Small World network structure to Scale Free networks, which employ the dynamics of "phase change" and "power laws" to create networks in which clusters come together to form "hubs". This "hub" structure means that 1) many nodes are "preferentially attached" to the hub and can efficiently share information and ideas with the hub, where competitive pressures will weed out the best ones, and 2) all the nodes in the network are separated only by a few degrees from each other, so repatriating synthesized information back from the hub to any given node is quick and cost efficient. For example, molecular networks in cells are characterized by four degrees of separation among hundreds of molecules, and even the human brain, with its many trillions of synaptic links between neuronal nodes, has neural networks that are separated by only four to five degrees, though admittedly the brain is less of a Scale Free network than a cell is. In both cases, it is essential for hubs in those networks to collect information from many thousands of sources, distill or synthesize it, and send communications back out to the original information sources.

Nevertheless, Nature is judicious about the risks it takes, and Scale Free networks carry with them a greater risk of failure than Small World networks do, so Scale Free networks are used sparingly and strategically. The human brain system is certainly one of the most prominent examples of how Nature designs a network that enjoys the best of both worlds. On the one hand, the human brain system resembles a Small World structure of highly networked neurons, glia cells, neural circuits, and functional systems that share all sorts of information very rapidly and broadly; it is also amazingly adaptive and "plastic", able to repurpose certain clusters of neurons and neural networks in the event of failure in other networks and systems. (For example, cortical regions of blind people that are normally used to process visual stimuli can be repurposed to more acutely process auditory stimuli, even allowing blind people to "see" sounds in ways that sighted people cannot.) On the other hand, the human brain system retains characteristics of Scale Free structure, being organized hierarchically, which means that certain functions and systems can be operationally prioritized and process certain critical information sets within the relevant network or system faster than would be possible in a Small World structure.

In Nature's self-organization information processing networks, especially with the human brain system itself, the biggest risks involve information leak and network failure. Basically, there are four fundamental threats to the integrity of information transfer in these networks: 1) random node/link failure, 2) cascading node/link failure, 3) random node/link attack (from outside agencies), and 4) directed node/cluster attack. In both Small World and Scale Free networks, random node failure does not represent a serious risk, but cascading failure is another matter. Because they have many different smaller clusters, Small World networks are highly "redundant", and if one or two clusters fail, the information flow within the network can be offloaded to other, often homogenous, clusters. However, as more cluster failures pile up, increasing the load on each remaining one, a previously redundant Small World network begins to look like a Scale Free network of a few hubs, and if one of those hubs fails, the entire network can go down. The well-known cascading failures of Small World network structure built into electrical energy grids are perfect examples, as was the debacle of the financial institution failures in 2008.

External attack is another story, however. If it is random, both the redundant nature of Small World networks and the fundamental concentration strength of Scale Free networks will protect them from collapse. On the other hand, a directed attack on Scale Free networks like the Web (e.g., attack on the Google web site) can disrupt or cripple it in short order. Clearly, it would take longer to bring down a Small World network, as the attack would need to target a larger number of (smaller) clusters to cause the "cascading failure", and it probably would have to be geared toward starting with the largest, most strategic clusters first. An attack on a Scale Free network, whose critical hubs usually self-identify quite easily, would not have to be as strategically planned.

When it comes to the human brain system and the whole notion of networked thinking, we will want to be equally mindful of not just cascading failure or escalating attack, but also of *cascading innovation.* As discussed in Chapter Eight, networked thinking seeks to leverage information that is prioritized within Scale Free networks, then disseminated by Small World ones, in such a way as to generate new concepts, ideas, and innovative thinking. The key to this leveraging process is learning how to creatively manipulate networked sets and patterns of information. In fact, that is precisely how I derived my concept of networked thinking in the first place—by playing with the possible connections between and among the information and concepts embedded in complexity science, network science, neuroscience, and Information Theory. For example, intriguing parallels exist among the statistical mechanics of Information Theory the power laws underlying preferential attachment in Scale Free networks, and the emergent processes through which certain emotions, feelings, and thoughts establish prominence in the human mind.

Non-structural Network Dynamics

Network structure certainly dictates many of the key information flow dynamics of networks, but that is not the end of the story. For example, network nodes may not just fail and suddenly disappear but might evolve, fail slowly, or change character in ways that shift the dynamics within the network. Similarly, network links may become rearranged in several dimensions, as for example in the case of a directed link that at one time only transferred information in one direction but is later repurposed to only transfer information in the other direction. (This also happens to be one of the key features of electrical engineering and computing.) And certainly, different kinds of networks take on their own sets of dynamics, so it is important to distinguish organic networks from material ones, tangible networks from intangible ones (like social networks), human ones from non-human ones. For example, human agency involves the dynamics of human "contexts"—social identities, preferences, affiliations, participation in groups, and the like, all of which would directly impact how people in a social or professional network share information. Some will share information and knowledge freely, some will not; some will respond quickly to information requests from within the network, some will not; some will seek or be willing to supply only certain types of information.

There is another aspect of electrical engineering that contains parallels to information flow dynamics in networks, especially personal ones. In social and professional networks, the configuration of directed and undirected links not only determines what information flows between nodes and in which direction, but also plays a role in impeding the flow of information within node clusters and sub-networks. Just as resistance is used to impede energy flow in electrical circuits, information flow in social and professional networks may be slowed or stopped by various forms of human "resistance". As discussed in Part II, our brain systems are hardwired in ways that generate both efficiencies and impedance, whether that involves computational issues or more complex cases of bias. And the information processing networks embedded in our brain systems have almost as many "inhibitory" neurons that can shut down links and information flow within networks as they do "excitatory" ones to move information along. Moreover, neurotransmitters in the human brain system can cause networks to cascade, giving rise to dominant thoughts, feelings, and behaviors. When electrochemical signals traveling along an "expectant" network reach a key threshold and cause it to "spike", information transfer takes place, and when the information flowing through a given network of networks "tips", discrete mental and behavioral outputs result.

What contributes to these spiking and cascading dynamics in the human brain system, in the form of information flows, probably has parallels within the dynamics of social and professional networks as well. In other words, although it is not often clear why some information flows quickly through a social network or certain ideas "tip" and cascade through professional networks, we know that they do so with great regularity. As relates to the Knowledge Networks discussed in Chapter Nine, this can be a significant factor, because it seems to require proactive management of not only network structure but information input and operational flows.

Finally, different types of networks also have different types of histories. As is the case with self-organizing systems, the networks that self-organize within such systems are functions of their operational histories. What has happened in the past within networks affects the current structural dynamics of those networks, just as those structural dynamics drive what will happen within them going forward. In this sense, it is similar to the dynamics of the human brain system and mind, for the structure and operation of a given brain clearly affects what goes on in the mind, just as the contents and decisions made in the mind eventually alter the very structure of the brain from which it emerges. Another way of looking at this phenomenon is through the lens of Einstein's Relativity—four dimensional spacetime is foundational to the formation of matter, but once created, that matter is what curves the very spacetime within which it manifests. It should certainly come as no surprise that the information processing networks of the human brain system are functions of their operating histories.

So at this point, network science has managed to provide a number of insights that prove useful in the practice of networked thinking and the development of Knowledge Networks: 1) real networks (organic, naturally forming ones) are constantly exposed to Random Information but there is no randomness, or "accident", in the way such networks are formed and evolve, especially those that self-organize within complex systems and particularly those "designed" by Nature; 2) as links between nodes are added in partially randomized networks, or as growth occurs in real networks, natural clusters begin to form; 3) these naturally forming clusters eventually create Small World networks, which reflect the primary structures of self-organizing networks; 4) many real networks are subjected to forms of preferential attachment, which give rise to power laws and Scale Free network structures; 5) network structures evolve, affected by the information flow dynamics within them, just as those information flows are influenced by network structures; and 6) network structures and information flows have histories, which affect their dynamics going forward. As will be discussed in Chapter Seven, all of these structural and non-structural network dynamics apply as apply to the neural networks of the human brain system as they do to any other real network.

Information Flow

Different types of networks—physical, organic, intangible, and personal—necessarily deal with different information sets and patterns. Personal networks involve human agency and therefore process the most complex array of information forms—express and implied, verbal and non-verbal, immediate and proposed, factual and speculative, and so forth—all of which flow through a particular network at different times, by varied means, and with unpredictable results. For example, in a professional network of experienced lawyers, if certain information that was considered confidential was identified as such and shared within the network, there would be no need to include additional information on the restricted use of such information, as it would be well implied. On the other hand, in a professional network of engineers in which proprietary knowledge is exchanged, it might be necessary to also share information about the expected use of that proprietary knowledge.

In personal networks, information flow dynamics can also be impacted by a number of other social and economic factors, such as cultural legacy, personality, and perspective. Sometimes information generated from one cultural legacy or experiential perspective does not translate into another, making information exchange difficult. Language barriers and cultural context also slow down information exchange, whether the network in question involves a group of university professors or the logistical components of an international goods shipment.

Additionally, as pointed out in the last chapter, information flow can be significantly impacted by message clarity. Noisy, ambiguous messages, particularly in personal networks, flow awkwardly at best, and at worst they can wreak all sorts of havoc. For example, take the often challenging information exchanges between an ex-husband and ex-wife in matters such as the disciplining of a child with whom they share custody. First, you have the usual Information Theory dynamics of message clarity and disruptive noise—the parents are divorced for a reason, probably have different communication styles, and doubtless have conflicting agendas that influence the message exchange between them. Then you add in a few scoops of heated emotion, stir, blend in the aftereffects of a related conversation between one of the ex's and his or her current spouse, and wait for a few seconds—well, you get the picture, and it's the sort of thing that happens with some frequency in personal networks.

In terms of the neural networks within the human brain system, information flow is largely determined and defined by factors such as the types of neurons that form the network links, the neuron/link length, the transfer speeds of sent signals (from synaptic firings and post-synaptic recovery times), and the recursive characteristics of the network, mitigated by inhibitory and excitatory neurons. More on this in Part II.

Environmental Context

Network structural dynamics and information flow are also necessarily affected by environmental context, which includes not only the specific conditions and exigencies that are bearing down on the network at any particular moment, but the historical context of the network environment as well. For example, because social systems generate considerable pressure to maintain one's social status, social networks are implicitly governed by the applicable norms of social convention within that system. We find ourselves complying with social norms and behavioral conventions precisely because we want to preserve our social status. Networks operating in social clubs, professional associations, and even religious institutions, all rely on this form of environmental context to establish their normative behaviors.

As it applies to information processing networks in the human brain system and the dynamics of networked thinking, the most relevant aspects of environmental context are the emergent phenomena generated by the brain system itself. The emergent human mind and the thoughts it produces are volatile, occasionally even chaotic—sometimes, without even understanding why, we find ourselves thinking the craziest things, which more than likely disrupt the working dynamics of our brain's neural networks as long as they linger.

At a more granular level, these brain systems and information processing networks are influenced by internal environmental factors such as temperature and biochemistry. Biochemistry in the brain plays a major role in the synaptic behaviors of neurons, especially within networks. Inordinately high temperatures, from various sources of inflammation, and abnormal swelling from concussions or other traumas, will break down and scramble the normal operational mechanics of the brain's neural networks. Even the spreading of memes, as described in the previous chapter, has a major impact on what information flows through the human brain system's networks and how they are restructured by such flows. For example, the "Golden Rule" (treat others as you would like to be treated yourself) is a cultural meme that speaks directly to the types of behaviors we end up imitating and how they will, over time, implicitly influence a wide range of our behaviors and thoughts. How that ultimately impacts what goes on in our brains is an open and interesting question, one that requires a deeper appreciation for what our human brain systems are like and how they work, which is the subject of Part II.

PART II—THE HUMAN BRAIN SYSTEM

4

OPERATIONAL MECHANICS OF THE SELF-ORGANIZING HUMAN BRAIN SYSTEM

Operational mechanics and dynamics of the human brain system

To gain a deeper understanding of our brains and how they operate as self-organizing systems, we should start by looking at the key elements of their detail and dynamic complexity. If the human body is itself the universe's most complex self-organizing system we know of, the human brain is surely the body's most complex subsystem. The human body has over 50 trillion cells, some of which are undergoing 20,000 to 100,000 chemical events a second, all as part of an adaptive process that allows the body to repair itself and thrive in a physical environment that is constantly changing. Given that the brain is highly integrated into the larger system of the body, with all its amines, peptides, and enzymes, the biochemistry of the human brain system operates in a complex cause and effect relationship with a number of subsystems of the body. For example, the signal sent to the body's adrenal glands to generate cortisol, in response to a perceived threat in the external environment, originates in the brain, but cortisol produced by adrenal glands eventually flows back into the brain, which then sets up a feedback system that ultimately modulates the original signal.

Adding further to its dynamic complexity, the human brain system contains many different kinds of cells, which serve various functions. The primary workhorse cells are the approximately 100 billion neurons (nerve cells) that "communicate" with each other by way of trillions of synaptic connections. (Neurons form the most important communication network in the brain, thanks to the presence of myelinated axons, which form the basis of its "white matter", while neuronal cell bodies and dendrites, supported by a network of glial cells, make up the brain's "grey matter". Axons

61

of a single neuron can extend themselves considerable distances within brain, linking up with thousands of different dendrites from other neurons to form very dynamic networks.) Synapses are the gaps (clefts) that exist between the ends of one neuron's axons, or transmitter sites, and other neurons' dendrites, or receiver sites. When these synapses "fire"— that is, undergo electrochemically driven information transfer across the synaptic gap—they effectively link neurons together into an active network, for a period of time that can range from milliseconds to hours.

Another element of dynamic complexity surfaces from the varying computational speeds that emerges from synaptic firing between neurons. The average brain can perform around 10 billion operations per second and absorb approximately 400 million bits of information per second, though "working memory", where conscious processing takes places, can only handle about 2500 bits per second. (Though there are no clear mechanical delineations between the "conscious" and "unconscious" activities of the human brain system, it is easy to see from the limits of working memory capacity that most of the information processed in the human brain system is not immediately available to the "conscious mind".) A good measure of the brain's operations and information processing activities take place in subcortical regions that are extraordinarily efficient in performing parallel processing of information. They are also not slowed down by having to connect with the many cortical areas that handle cognitive processing, with all of their intricate feedforward and feedback systems, which provide critical updates on changing conditions in the external environment.

Because some neurons carry hundreds of dendrites, each one of which can potentially create a potential synaptic gap with an axon of another neuron, the number of potential synaptic connections among all of the brain's neurons may be in the quadrillions, and of course the permutations and combinations of neuronal connections that can be formed into actual *networks* is virtually limitless. Mapping all of these networks within specific time frames would seem to be virtually impossible. Nevertheless, we do know that these neural networks do most of the brain's "computing" (primarily analogue parallel processing, differing from digital computers), using neurons that are capable of both *encoding and transmitting* data/information, which is why the human brain is so much more powerful and versatile than any man made machine. Interestingly, the next major leap in commercial computing is likely to come from the design of "memristors", which would be able to replicate in some fashion the neuron's dual encoding and transmitting functionality and obviate the need of current computers to create separate processors for each function.

The human brain system uses "inhibitory" and "excitatory" neurons to manage both the "firing" speed of synapses and the formation of networks. The primary inhibitory neuron is called "GABA", and it serves to put the brakes on the synaptic activity and modulate the formation of specific neural connections, networks, and circuits. In contradistinction, excitatory neurons use different types of neurotransmitters to drive electrochemical signaling between neurons and even predispose certain neurons to link together. In order for synapses to fire, the electrical signals traveling through a given neuron must reach a certain threshold, which factors significantly into the network dynamics of the human brain's many neuronal connections. As pointed out in Chapter Two, when these networked connections reach critical thresholds, or "tipping points", they often cascade into a particular set of information distribution configurations and dynamics. In the human brain system, timing is everything, not only with respect to the firing of synapses but also to achieving the necessary threshold for neurons to connect into any given network, as well as to maintain the integrity of that network going forward.

The coordinated and synchronized firing of certain neurons that give rise to predisposed networks allows the human brain system to form 1) critical feedforward and feedback systems, and 2) historical records (stored outside of conscious awareness) that serve important cognitive functions such as memory, prediction, and rationalizing of otherwise dissonant pieces of information. For example, Split-Brain research has established that an "interpreter" emerges within the unified mind that keeps a running narrative of what "makes sense", so that the mind maintains a plausible explanation for things and thereby retains some measure of equilibrium, even in the presence of what might seem to be incompatible pieces of information.

Detail and dynamic complexity also define the mechanics of the human brain system's self-organizing development. The average human at birth has around 100 billion neurons, grows another 100 billion in the first six months of life, then weans out half of that total over the next year, following the general principal that neurons that form into viable networks increase the strength of their network connections with use, while those that do not eventually die away. This developmental process continues to a lesser extent until around age 25, with the primary functional change occurring in the pre-frontal cortex, which does not fully mature until the late teens or early twenties, which is the primary reason teenagers are so "concrete" in their thinking, often lacking the capacity to appreciate nuance and complexity.

The key driver of this development process, and the major lever of change, comes from the complex dynamics of gene expression, although certainly randomness factors into the equation. Whether influencing the initial formation of basic brain systems structures during gestation, driving the maturation process during early childhood, or fine-tuning the self-assembly that takes place for another 20 years, gene expression both contributes to the organizational configuration of the overall system and guides its operational dynamics. Sometimes such gene expression is catalyzed by epigenetic factors, flowing out of the many different forms of internal and external "conditions" to which a given brain system is subjected over time. In many cases, such internal and external conditions are determined by what the brain system "attends to" at any given moment, which results in the sequenced expression of genes that continue to drive the adaptive responses of the integrated brain system. There is still much we need to learn, however, about how thoughts and other mental states in the mind affect gene expression, and the investigation of the human epigenome and how it factors into gene expression within the human brain system has only just begun.

As an integrated system, the human brain should be understood as an *analog* parallel processor, which processes information, then "learns" and adapts by first making predictions from that information and then comparing those predictions to imputed or computed outcome. What the human brain system imputes is obviously a key component of not only its adaptive nature but its functional capacity as well. In the typical non-linear cause and effect dynamics of self-organizing systems, what the brain imputes, or "perceives"—both in terms of incoming sensory stimuli and internal mental representations—affects what it can attend to and process, just as what it attends to affects what it next imputes and perceives. Accordingly, the human brain system is highly influenced by what is "present" to it at any given moment, including what the brain system has just been conditioned to look for. And certainly this is one of those domains of brain system mechanics where it can be said that "as goes the brain, so goes the mind". In other words, the default perspective of the human brain system and mind tends to make them "prisoners of the moment", inclined to perceive and think about the next moment through the lens of the last one. In general, the human brain system tends to process new information by comparing and contrasting it to information recalled from the brain's memory systems, then extrapolates from past experience to predict future events, calibrate perception, and drive various states of consciousness. In essence, the virtuous information processing loop works as follows: *perception—attention—information processing—memory—consciousness—perception.*

Perception is therefore both a key component of the human brain's functional systems and a significant factor in how both the human brain and mind calibrate "reality". For example, visual and perceptual consciousness emerge from processing of stimuli in specific cortical areas, using feedback loops to construct images from the millions of information bits originally received in the retina and transmitted by the retinal nerve. But because there are not enough cells in the retina to absorb all the data of a given image, the systems for processing visual stimuli must fill in some of the gaps and construct a *representation* of the image, using different tools such as memory and logic.

Accordingly, in every experience of visual consciousness and perception, the human brain, as a complex system, necessarily creates visual *illusions.* We know that we do not actually see *all* the details of what lies in front of our eyes, which leaves open the possibility that, in some cases more than others, our brains may fill in more information from its own memory banks than, excluding significant details that actually exist within the particular visual field, leading to an emergent, perhaps even adaptive, "perceived reality". This is particularly true in emotionally charged situations, where the brain system will pull in emotionally evaluated memories that correspond to the sensory stimuli confronting it and most likely derive an interpretation of those stimuli that to some extent further distorts the perceived reality. This aspect of the human brain system's dynamics complexity ultimately creates the most important characteristic of the human mind, as it relates to both thinking and interpersonal communication—everyone in the world has a different brain system, a mind of his/her own, and his/her own perception of "reality".

The human brain system is amazingly powerful and efficient, especially compared to artificial computing alternatives. The entire brain requires only about 10 to 25 watts of energy a second, considerably less than a computer would while performing similar processes, such as recognizing patterns of sound in voices or attempting to orient itself in time and space. Because the trillion cells making up the human brain system must fit into a small area (so that the human head can make it safely out of the female birth canal, which became smaller over time as our ancestors gained bipedal agility), it has managed to self-organize into a highly efficient information processing "hierarchical nested" network of the Small World networks. Due to these size constraints, as the human brain system evolved over the last 200,000 years, it gained new structures and functions primarily due to changes in its network structure, and recently neuroscientists have discovered that increases in network formation and development of Small World network structures are also what most distinguishes young brains from mature ones (particularly between ages 12 and 25).

In spite of its structural and operational efficiencies, the human brain is still an energy hog, making up only around 2% of the human body's total weight but consuming over 20% of its energy output. For better and worse, depending on the situation, our energy efficient brain systems have also generated a number of "shortcuts". Some of these heuristics and biases, many of which present serious obstacles to networked thinking, are discussed at the end of this chapter.

Now let us step back and take a high level view of the human brain system. As a subsystem within the larger system of the human body, the brain system essentially fulfills four fundamental functions, using three basic areas of the brain—the brain stem and cerebellum, middle brain/limbic system, and cortical areas. The cerebellum, located at the back of the brain, and the brain stem, which is evolutionarily the oldest and least complex part of the brain, take care of bodily functions and regulate the autonomic nervous system; the cerebellum has the additional purpose of controlling key aspects of motor coordination—primarily by way of feedback systems—and interestingly, even though it makes up only 10% of the brain's total volume, it contains 40% of its neurons. As noted earlier, the functional capacity of the human brain is not measured as much by the quantity of neurons in any given region as by the neuronal interconnections that exist, the processing speeds within those networks, and the way those networks are also connected to other regions and functional areas of the brain. Accordingly, neo-cortical regions in the front of the brain that are responsible for generating fast assessments, accurate predictions, and effective judgments of a given situation or condition, may actually be networked in such a way as to produce more computational power than the cerebellum, even though they contain fewer neurons.

Next, an area in the middle of the brain, which includes the basal ganglia, hypothalamus, hippocampus, amygdala, and thalamus (often referred to as the "limbic system"), plays the role of alert system, generating the "fight or flight" instincts; it is also the system that processes emotions, regulates motivation, and forms new memories, though the storage of those emotions and memories is thought to be more widely distributed throughout other regions of the brain.

This centralized area of the brain also hosts some of its most important feedforward and feedback systems, known as "thalamocortical nuclei", which contain a large number of pyramidal neurons that extend up through the six layers of cortex that lines the upper surface of the brain. These nuclei help to integrate various functions within the human brain system, like processing sensory stimuli, modulating cognitive response, and directing motor control, which clearly demand considerable amounts of information feedback.

One interesting feature of this centralized collection of functional brain systems emerges from its high level of interconnectivity with structures within the neo-cortex, where complex cognition takes place, including the use of logic and reason. This interconnectivity means that emotions, which are essentially the effect of biochemical events within the limbic system resulting from the processing of sensory stimuli, necessarily infuse all thoughts with some emotional content, thereby giving rise to the phenomenon we think of as "feelings". (While most people conflate emotions and feelings, neuroscience treats them quite differently, and when it comes to the subject of human thinking, it is useful to keep this distinction in mind. Whereas emotions are products of brain biochemistry, feelings could be considered "emotion based thoughts".) Essentially, that means that there is no such thing as purely rational thought, whether or not we might actually be aware of the associated emotion that is connected to any given thought. Accordingly, to the extent possible, we should seek to identify, acknowledge, and manage our emotions before making judgments and decisions, and this is basically what "emotional intelligence" is all about.

The last major functional component of the human brain system is found in the cortex (including the sub-cortex and neo-cortex), which houses all of the complex systems for cognitive functioning, including integrated sensory processing; coordinating motor functioning; engaging in complex reasoning, thinking, and judgment; managing emotion, motivation, and disappointment; all forms of planning; and of course complex decision making. The cortex also contains recently developed systems that give rise to our "social brain", the sophisticated sentinel that helps us navigate our highly complex social world. The neo-cortex is a relatively recent evolutionary addition that effectively provides us with many important aspects of mind that particularly distinguish the human species, including strategic thinking, self-awareness, and critical aspects of motivation and intention.

For apparent reasons of systems redundancy and leverage, the human brain system is divided into both right and left hemispheres, which are connected by "cables" of neurons called the corpus callosum. While there are some structural and functional differences between the generally parallel systems of each hemisphere, they also operate in a complex interrelationship, as Split-Brain research has catalogued over the last half century. Most of the brain's functional systems have counterparts in each hemisphere, but there is some functional specialization as well, particularly when it comes to language. This interesting structural phenomenon offers useful insight into the complex nature of the human brain and its approach to information processing efficiency, redundancy, and leverage. It also provides some very useful insights into the nature of the emergent human mind, as discussed in Chapter Six.

Over the last several decades, neuroscientists have been able to use fMRI and PET scans, as well as EEG readouts, to identify specific areas in the brain, such as the amygdala, hippocampus, hypothalamus, basal ganglia, and nucleus accumbens, which offer evidence of being discrete but highly integrated functional systems. With this evidence, it now seems possible to construct a view of the complex adaptive human brain system defined by two integrated, but distinct higher level systems: 1) a highly self-referential system located toward the rear of the brain that acts as a default mechanism for processing and responding to incoming stimuli and internal thoughts, and which unfortunately tends to dominate the contents of our conscious minds; and 2) a synthesizer system in the front of the brain that acts more like an objective third party, able to escape from well-entrenched associated memories and make thoughtful choices, "free" from all the history of recorded experiences that so powerfully drive the self-referential system. The details of these systems are discussed further in Chapter Seven and captured in Figure 4.

Because of its nested network structure, the human brain system is highly effective as a predictive machine and very efficient as an information processor, even though all its different functional networks are not necessarily optimally cobbled together, given the way things have evolved in the brains of our ancestors over the last 200,000 years. (No doubt, given a clean sheet of paper, network scientists or engineers would design the human brain system quite differently, but then again, philosophers might want to take their own completely different approach! In any event, the human brain system is what it is, and yet we know that it is possible for us to consciously change how it works, both in the near term and more permanently over time.)

We know, for example, that the human brain system can reallocate the use of certain neurons to different functions and relegate some rote functions to subcortical regions for automatic processing, which is often referred to as "hard-wiring", thereby freeing up the cortex for other cognitive functions. That is what happens, for example, when you learn to ride a bike or drive a car. The brain is also highly "plastic", meaning it can add information to an existing set of neural networks, as well as "rewire" existing networks and systems so as to produce an entirely different output, as, for example, occurs in the development of a new thought. (Interestingly, the brains of blind people have even been observed to convert neuronal circuits within areas dedicated to process visual stimuli to the processing of auditory stimuli, in some cases allowing them to "see" certain sounds.) It is because of the brain's tremendous plasticity that we are able to reform memories, learn new skills, modify our belief systems, and alter our behaviors, all essential elements of the human brain's functionality as an adaptive system.

Because it has so much to do and such a large amount of information to process, the human brain system uses two key mechanisms to do its work, both of which are quite relevant to the process of networked thinking. First, the brain "chunks" data and information, in much the same way that digital information networks "packetize" data, although the brain system's chunks of information can be either digital or analogue. The human brain system has many different ways of segregating and tagging these information chunks, in order to most efficiently manipulate them into increasingly large, coherent chunks, which is critical to optimal brain function, given the energy costs involved in storing, retrieving, and distributing data/information throughout millions of networks.

Second, the human brain system tends to set up neural networks and circuits that "expect" to receive the same instructions and information over and over again, which has the effect of making those neural pathways stronger and more efficient at processing new information and signaling appropriate responses. Neuroscientists like to say "neurons that fire together, wire together", and they refer to this phenomenon as LTP, or long-term potentiation. At first glance, this phenomenon would seem to hinder the adaptive capacities of the brain, possibly even leading to "closed" systems within the brain's information processing systems (and therefore a closed mind as well), but the truth is that adaptation carries with it a very high energy cost, and so the brain must operate in a delicate balance, finding ways to save energy while continuing to adapt to ever increasing information flows and functional demands. In any event, in much the same way that the cells lining our stomach walls develop "expectations" about the kind of food chemistries it will have to digest, the human brain system carries "expectations" about the stimuli it will encounter, and without doubt, this lays the foundation for the many emotional and psychological expectations we all experience as we move through life.

Genomes, gene sequences, and the dynamics of gene expression affect not only the self-assembly but also the physical operation of the human brain system and its trillion different cells. Only 2% of our genes code for proteins, and most of the remainder serve regulatory roles, either turning on or off other genes, under different conditions and timing parameters, or otherwise directing the expression of genes within specific sets of environmental conditions. (For example, changes in internal body biochemistry or external sensory stimuli.) Fully 80% of the 23,000 genes in the human genome are expressed in the brain. The way in which genes are networked and expressed allows them to serve many different functions in the brain. Some genes act as "promoters", responsible for switching other genes on or off, under certain environmental conditions. Sometimes genes are only activated during certain periods of the human body's physical development. Or they may produce an enzyme that snips out parts of a protein created by another gene. But essentially genes contain the instructions for making proteins that form the building blocks of all the body's material, structural, and operational capabilities. In other words, whether operating alone or in some form of genetic network, genes carry instructions to make proteins that ultimately dictate a large measure of the human brain system's operating dynamics, whether that involves the production of neurotransmitters or the generating the many biochemical activities of 900 billion supporting glial cells. Equally importantly, as in the case of the brain system's self-organizing development, many different epigenetic phenomena make it possible for relevant genes to be expressed in response to certain changes in the body's or brain's internal or external environment, allowing it to remain a highly adaptive system.

Operational dynamics—brain heuristics and biases

Now that we have scoped out the major characteristics, functions, and structural components of the human brain system, it will be useful to review some of the key tendencies that emerge from these factors. While not by any means an exhaustive study, the material I have outlined below covers the heuristics and biases that are most relevant to the subject matter of networked thinking and to which we often fall prey if we are not vigilant.

Heuristics

Millions of years of evolutionary pressures, especially the last 100,000, during which our species has lived in some form of social system, have caused the human brain system to develop many different operational characteristics. At this juncture in our evolutionary development, we have indeed become an interesting, complex species, especially in terms of our behavior in groups, organizations, and societies. On the one hand, we are the only species with self-reflective consciousness—we are aware that we are aware of our own space, identity, and capacity for agency in the world. On the other hand, much of our behavior is often driven by some fundamental brain "heuristic"—fast acting tendencies, or cognitive shortcuts, probably numbering in the hundreds—that in some cases we have shared with our primate ancestors for perhaps as much as 35 million years. For example, recent studies have shown that capuchin monkeys, whose last common ancestors with humans lived around 35 million years ago, are predisposed to loss aversion and reference dependence in much the same way that humans are. In other words, like humans, they demonstrate behavior that is more concerned with what might be lost in a given choice than what might be gained, and, like us, they are also highly influenced in their choices by how the resulting output affects their situation in reference to the circumstances of others, rather than the net effect results, in absolute terms.

As we have seen, the human brain system is both a central information processor for most of the body's functions and a unique *thinking machine,* which means it has many more demands on its operations than it has the energy and time to fully attend to, so it has to create many different types of shortcuts in both its cognitive and non-cognitive processing activities. (Most of these heuristics would be associated with Daniel Kahneman's "fast acting" System 1, or what I refer to as the Default system, as discussed further in Chapter Seven.) The less aware we are of these heuristics, the more they tend to drive our thoughts and behaviors, usually outside our awareness.

In terms of their effect on the development of compelling networked thinking, the most relevant and significant human brain system heuristics, and the consequent effects that they have on the emergent human mind include:

- Familiarity and Default
  Because it carries certain needs to chunk data and information in such a way as to construct actual images, representations, and symbols of an "external reality", the human brain system defaults to a process of "object" identification and representation. These "objects" are used over and over, which eventually leads to all sorts of rote and instinctual behaviors. For example, a family member represents a certain "object" that is associated with kinship and gives rise to instinctual inclination to defend any given family member, regardless of the facts and circumstances. This heuristic also helps explain why so many people resist change, maintain their fixed belief systems, are attracted to "sound bites" (especially in political ads!), and continue to do what they have always done, even it does not produce the results they claim to be seeking.

- Clarity
  Because of the way the human brain system chunks data and information in order to create "objects", it struggles to process information that is fundamentally large in size or remote in physical or virtual distance, so it seeks out information that presents a clear picture. This heuristic explains why so many people seek simple, short-term solutions and engage in concrete, compartmentalized thinking, while trying to avoid ambiguous issues, foreign cultures, and events taking place in faraway places. (See Chapter Five.)

- Availability
  The more recent (and therefore available to working memory) an example or analogy is, the more compelling it is to our human brain systems and conscious minds. This heuristic factors into what happens not only within our brain system's many feedback systems but also within its millions of discrete information processing networks. Clearly it has parallel impact within the dynamics of networked thinking, and in particular the Knowledge Networks discussed in Chapter Nine.

- Scarcity
  Because the human brain system consumes a great deal of energy *all the time*, it is highly sensitized to receiving adequate blood supply, oxygen, and glucose. Both the brain and the emergent mind react powerfully to sensations of scarcity, and interestingly the mind exaggerates its perception of scarcity if it senses a restriction on its "freedom". This heuristic explains why so many people operate from a psychology and emotional base of scarcity rather than abundant generosity, which affects everything from their general behaviors in social and professional networks to their levels of cooperation in "game theory" scenarios. On a more trivial level, it also explains why our brains and minds catalogue things that are rare as "valuable". (The converse is true as well—if cultural norms consider something "valuable", people of that culture think of it as rare.)

- Basic needs
  The human brain system is clear about how it organizes its approach to satisfying its basic needs. Energy obviously comes first, so food is always a high priority, and forever on our minds. Moreover, as the human brain system evolved over the last 50,000 years, with the advent of more organized social systems and particularly the emergence of specialized skills, it "learned" to confabulate food with money, fairness, and social status. That is why food, money, and social status drive so much of our thinking and behavior.

Because our species is so highly "socialized", our brain systems also carry a set of "moral heuristics". We (and even some of our primate cousins like chimpanzees) are hardwired to be compassionate and empathetic. Deep down, our minds understand that if social order breaks down, our very survival is threatened, and so we instinctively learn to cooperate and collaborate with each other. Our brain systems and minds have moved beyond even these instincts, having developed a set of moral, value based "short cuts" as well. Many of these moral heuristics are embedded in our legal system and different ethical codes.

For example, all human societies, and the legal systems that emerge within them, balance their judgment of behavior based on two sets of criteria—the end result, and the intention behind the behavior in question. Apparently, due to the exigencies of early human societies, and even those of our primate ancestors, establishing normative behavior and punishing aberrant behavior had to be based on one thing—the consequence, or end result. Intention was considered secondary or even irrelevant. Survival of the species depended on social cohesion, which depended on a fixed code of acceptable behaviors, reflected in legal systems like the Napoleonic Code. As human society became more sophisticated and complex, behavioral nuances like the intention of the actor began to matter more, and legal systems started to punish bad intentions even in cases where the victims of such behavior suffered no harm. In any event, even today, different cultures have a wide range of attitudes toward this balance between end result of behavior and the intention behind it, so the brain systems that are impacted by those cultures tend to generate distinct sets of moral heuristics—sometimes the means justify the ends, sometimes the ends justify the means.

Predictably, our brain systems are now hardwired to apply both approaches, but because these approaches are nuanced by the dynamics of a particular situation, our brains and our minds get confused about when and where one approach should be applied rather than the other. Interestingly, based on genetic predispositions and environmental conditioning, some human brains have greater capacity than others to sort out moral dilemmas and avoid the confusion of when to judge/punish someone for intending to do "bad" things, regardless of the resulting outcome, and when to judge/punish him or her for simply being the causal "agent" of a "bad" thing, regardless of his or her intention. When time is short, our brains gravitate toward simple solutions and tend to operate more peremptorily, often producing inconsistent and confused moral judgments. So, just as the human brain heuristically gravitates toward information that is immediately available rather than information that has to be laboriously called up from memory systems, and just as the human brain struggles to distinguish between patterns of meaningful information and those that are entirely random or useless, it also tends to make quick moral judgments, based on past "experience", rather than tangle with the nuances of morality and ethics.

Biases

Closely aligned with heuristics in terms of how they cause the human brain system and our emergent minds to act peremptorily rather than in a considered fashion, biases can have a significant impact on information flow in social and professional networks and are therefore relevant to our pursuit of networked thinking and Knowledge Networks:

- Implicit association bias
  Essentially the source of what results in stereotyping, this bias is both deeply entrenched in the human brain system and well documented. (For a great read on this phenomenon, consult Malcolm Gladwell's discussion of the Harvard Implicit Association Test in *Blink.*) Different theories abound on why and how our brain systems acquired such profoundly rooted racial, ethnic, and physical associations, but most likely it all stems from our ancestors' days in tribal societies, when making distinctions between the faces of friend and foe was nothing short of a survival skill. Moreover, as pointed out in Chapter Seven, the human brain system's Default system relies heavily on the comparison, contrasting, and association of "objects", and it is easy to see why our brains carry implicit racial biases to this day. The whole implicit association bias continues to be an awkward topic in 21st century human society, but it seems clear that the bias exists and that the human brain system generates a significant measure of conscious and unconscious thoughts, feelings, and behaviors that are directly caused by it.
- Cognitive laziness bias
  Our brain systems are hardly "lazy", but they do like to follow the path of least resistance. All self-organizing systems seek to conserve energy and efficiently manage the "cost" of processing information, and the human brain system is no different. Unfortunately, the human mind, which emerges in part from the functional processes of the underlying human brain system, does become tired, overworked, and otherwise taxed to the point where it fails to consider

all of the new possible ways in which new information might be manipulated and interpreted to generate new thoughts and ideas.

- Negativity bias

   Because of its embedded aversion to loss, as discussed above, the human brain system carries a biased sensitivity toward information that threatens the realization of its intended or predicted goals. Accordingly, the human brain/mind tends to overemphasize the importance of "negative" information that seemingly threatens a particular prediction, goal, expectation, or desire. This bias significantly intrudes on thinking processes, because it tends to shut down important feedback systems that would encourage adaptive thinking.

- Control bias

   The human brain system is predisposed to operate in a "default" mode, using the resources of the Default system described in Chapter Seven, which favors an orientation toward "command and control". Interestingly, the more the human brain/mind "perceives" that it is in "control", the more "confidence" it gains. (The inverse is also true.) This means that our brain/minds are more likely to perpetuate thoughts and behaviors that lead to a sense of control, which can also generate serious overconfidence in our thinking.

- Future bias

   Because our brain systems are predictive machines, they are necessarily oriented toward what happens next and how accurate their predictions were. This bias toward future events points up a major difference between Default and Integrated thinking, discussed in Chapter Eight. The brain's Default system makes its predictions primarily by extrapolating from past experiences, but the Integrated system allows for more open-ended choice, based on the consideration of many different pieces of information. The more aware we are of these dynamics, the more our brain systems and minds can leverage this future bias to make wise, open-minded choices, rather than ones that simply reflect what was done in the past.

- Confirmation bias

   Just as it develops expectations of the stimuli it anticipates processing, the human brain system seeks out information that confirms what it already it "knows", and in this domain, as goes the brain, so goes the mind. When confirmation bias works hand in hand with negativity bias, they can have devastating effects on our thinking processes.

- Affirmation bias
  In order to insure survival and maintain social status, our brain systems implicitly process information and generate behaviors that they predict will be noticed by others. Affirmation bias plays a major role in the perpetuation of certain ideas and norms in human culture, by accentuating the selection and spreading of a given meme over another.

5

THE COMPLEX ADAPTIVE HUMAN BRAIN SYSTEM

By definition, any self-organizing system must also be complex and adaptive. Such complex adaptive systems are defined by their structural and operational dynamics, in particular their non-linear, hierarchical nature; their reliance on information networks; the importance of their feedforward and feedback systems; and their capacity for generating emergent phenomena or properties. Emergence occurs in a complex system when the system's component parts interact, generating something more than just the sum of those parts. As discussed in the next chapter, once they do emerge, these phenomena and systems properties may interoperate with various systems components and contribute to the adaptive dynamics of such systems. On the other hand, once these emergent phenomena do come into existence, they are necessarily constrained by the system's boundaries and characteristics, to much the same extent as the system's component parts are. For example, two hydrogen and one oxygen atom bond at room temperature in structures that cause water to remain liquid rather than crystalized, and the emergent property of "wetness" that characterizes this liquid state will endure until a phase change occurs.

Complex adaptive systems structural dynamics
Non-linearity

Complex adaptive systems are comprised of elements that operate in a non-linear, primarily *circular,* cause and effect relationship. In other words, as these elements interoperate within the system, it is often difficult to distinguish cause from effect, and this is particularly true with the human brain system. Does the firing of a certain neural network cause a thought to emerge, or is the thought generated by some other phenomenon, which then causes the firing of that specific neural network, which then allows the thought to be stored into short-term or long-term memory? Similar examples emerge within the significant self-organizing and complex adaptive systems of our lives, such as economic markets, ecological systems, and social relationships. Does a drop in market demand cause a reduction in supply, or is the dip in supply caused by some other phenomenon, such as a scarcity of requisite production materials, which then causes a chill in demand, as buyers seek alternatives to whatever is perceived to be short in supply? Do changes in the habitat of a species diminish its numbers, or is there some other cause, which then affects an entire food chain, and in turn, other aspects of that species' habitat, which then causes the reduction in that species' numbers? Do the thoughts or behaviors of one person alter the minds of an entire group, or does a new "groupthink" phenomenon emerge from some other agency, which in turn changes the behavior of each person within the group? Circular cause and effect dynamics is one of the most critical, and at the same time analytically challenging, aspects of complex adaptive systems, particularly the human brain system.

Various elements of brain information processing mechanics, like the type of neural network involved, the speed of synaptic connectivity, and impinging biochemistry, interoperate in a complex array of dynamics to process and store information. With current technology, it is almost impossible to sort out what elements cause which effects, or even if some phenomena are causes or effects. New techniques in optogenetics may soon be able to help neuroscientists sort out some of this non-linear complexity, but it will be a long time before we get a really clear picture, if ever. That said, using non-linear analytics from complexity science at least helps us identify important cause and effect relationships, model some possible structures, and develop credible hypotheses to test. Moreover, this systems approach can identify and account for chaotic factors, so as to avoid getting lost in a sea of seemingly random causes and effects.

Non-linear models can also help us better understand the interrelationship of brain and mind. There is still much debate among philosophers and scientists on the source and nature of the human mind, but there can be no doubt that certain aspects of mind emerge directly from the functional structure and operation of the human brain system. We experience feelings in our minds as a result of the way our brain systems bio-chemically process emotions and connect them to thoughts. As discussed in the next chapter, we even experience a subjective consciousness, sense of selfhood, agency, will, and intention in our minds precisely because of the way the human brain system sets up feedforward and feedback systems, in order to test its predictions, survive, and accomplish specific goals, as well as to maintain equilibrium within the entire system. And each time the human mind experiences these phenomena, it implicitly impinges on the mechanics of the brain systems from which the mind emerges, generating a very complex non-linear cause and effect relationship.

What happens in the human brain system, whether it involves natural, internal processes such as the management of strong emotions or the ingestion of foreign chemicals embedded in drugs, food, and alcohol, clearly impacts the condition of the mind, and the motivation, thoughts, and feelings that take place in it. In classic cause and effect non-linearity, changes in the structure and operational dynamics of the human brain system cause new effects within the mind, just as it is well accepted science now that by manipulating one's mind, through drugs, exercise, meditation, thought exercises, and the like, one can change the structure and functioning of one's brain. But again, sometimes it is hard to know whether changes within the brain system cause shifts in the mind, or shifts of the mind cause changes in the brain system.

Given the dynamics of chaotic systems and non-linearity in adaptive systems, they necessarily become increasingly complex and hierarchical, absent the injection of countermeasures. Chaotic systems provide a necessary, often rule-like process for breaking down and reframing the operational dynamics within a given system, then helping to "renormalize" it and enhance its adaptive capacities.

Hierarchy

Complex adaptive systems generate the intelligence to learn and adapt from both internal and external sources. Such learning is generated from information processing that takes place from both the bottom up and the top down. Accordingly, such systems must build and perpetuate a hierarchical structure, which allows them to both prioritize critical elements of adaptive intelligence and disseminate the learned intelligence, through feedforward/feedback systems (bottom up), and symbolizing that learning in the mind (top down). For example, when experience in an interpersonal relationship generates new intelligence on how to predict another person's future behavior, that intelligence is passed on to all sorts of different brain systems, to help adjust many conscious and unconscious thoughts and behaviors; at the same time, the mind makes certain assessments and judgments about that person's personality and ascribes some archetypal characteristics (using symbols) to that personality profile, for future reference. Or when someone learns a new physical skill, like a different technique for hitting a golf ball, that intelligence will become embedded in various cognitive and subcortical brain systems (as so called "muscle memory"), while at the same time making specific mental notes, such as "use a lighter grip" that will help recreate the technique the next time it is time to practice.

Top down hierarchical learning also originates from external sources. Human brain systems, and the emergent intelligence they create, are amazingly powerful, and we do not yet know exactly how learning gained from other people operates in a non-linear cause and effect relationship with the learning processes of (bottom up) internal systems, but we can be sure that they are interdependent. In like fashion, whatever intelligence and learning have been embedded in memes over the millennia must have some non-experiential and non-linear effect on our minds and thinking, even if we struggle to measure it accurately.

Complex adaptive systems operational dynamics
Information Networks

Complex adaptive systems thrive on information flow, both internally and from the external environment. Information from the environment injects new "ideas" into the system, updates predictive mechanisms, and provides valuable feedback on the effectiveness of the system's predictive strategies. All complex adaptive systems are "open", because they continually receive information from their environments and adapt to changes within them, which also means that they are inevitably subjected to the tug of entropy—the never-ending march toward some sort of equilibrium state. Unlike the measures that complex systems take to maintain equilibrium within their internal operational mechanics, entropy is an exogenous force, an elusive and subtle factor that tends to unwind ordered structures, from atomic and molecular systems to entire galaxies of star systems. The laws of thermodynamics tell us that "Work", in the form of energy and information, is required to maintain ordered structure within a complex system. Information networks therefore play a major role in staving off disorganizing influences within complex adaptive systems, especially the human brain system.

Feedforward and feedback systems

Informational networks in complex adaptive systems like the human brain not only process internally and externally sourced data and information but distribute the synthesized outputs of that processing to all the system's subsystems. In order to be adaptive, a complex system must be making predictions, processing feedback, "learning" from the results of that feedback, and undertaking adaptive responses from that learning. In other words, the goals of the complex adaptive system's many prediction generating subsystems must be "fed forward" into the many different subsystems that execute a command and/or feed information back from the results of an executed command. When a pang of hunger taps into a memory system that reminds the appropriate sensorimotor systems to pick up a piece of food laying within reaching distance, feedforward processes are initiated, then quickly followed by all sorts of tactile and visionary feedback, perhaps even ending in a sense of satiation from the original hunger pang.

While feedforward systems send messages about goals, predictions, and other specific instructions, feedback systems return messages that are either "positive" or "negative". Positive messages reinforce the existing systems dynamics and their designated outputs. For example, the various feedback systems involved in the process of eating described above would visually and tactilely confirm attainment of the desired goal of picking up the food, and sensors in the tongue and stomach would confirm that it was good food or not, and so on, until the conscious mind was satisfied that no additional action was required to satiate the hunger. So just as a thermostat sends positive feedback to keep a heating system going until the desired temperature has been reached and negative feedback messages when it has been, so the brain will keep sending messages to the sensorimotor system to reach for more food until it receives the messages back from its own biochemical state that enough food has been consumed. (As we all know too well, sometimes the lag in these negative feedback messages is considerable and they come too late, after we have already consumed far more than we needed to!)

Constraints

Non-adaptive, ordered systems place identifiable constraints on its operational elements (or agents), while chaotic systems contain no such constraints. Within complex adaptive systems, on the other hand, the system elements or agents and the system itself constrain one another, which makes it difficult to accurately predict what will happen within the system over time. For example, in the complex adaptive system of a market economy, the capital markets represent one system element that will not only contain its own adaptive dynamics, which affect the daily cost of capital, but will also generate various constraints within the larger economic system that will affect its growth, such as the availability of capital for growing companies or the cost of mortgages for prospective homeowners. In parallel fashion, the variations in supply and demand for various goods, international trade surpluses or deficits, and other such economic factors will serve to constrain various elements within the capital markets system, such as currency exchange rates. Clearly, these types of systems constraints make predicting precise movements in either the capital markets or the market economy challenging, if not impossible.

Constraints within the human brain system take many forms, from the quantum physics and organic chemistry of the body's biochemistry to the mechanics of gene expression and synaptic firing speeds. And as will be discussed in the next chapter, what constrains the human brain system invariably constrains the emergent human mind, as well as the thinking it engenders.

6

EMERGENT PHENOMENA IN THE COMPLEX
ADAPTIVE HUMAN BRAIN SYSTEM

Emergent Phenomena

As any biologist, neuroscientist, or even complexity scientist would tell you, every human brain system is unique. Of course, your common sense would tell you the same thing, once you thought about the dynamics of self-organization. Moreover, if we imagine the human brain system as a highly dynamic *network*, in which each neuron can be constantly changing its links to other neurons, firing at varying speeds, and forever altering the nature of the system's information sharing structures, how could we ever doubt that every human brain system is unique? It also follows that if every human brain system is unique, then so should every phenomenon and property that emerges from each such system. Every human mind, aspect of consciousness, set of perceptions and perspectives, belief system, and so on would have its own individual characteristics. No two people could ever experience life the same way.

Given this reality, it's not hard to see why the true beauty of the human complex adaptive brain system lies not as much in its structural dynamics as in its capacity for generating "emergent phenomena". And while uniqueness of complex physical systems presents intriguing implications, uniqueness of the phenomena that emerge from them is simply, well, mind boggling. Just contemplating what goes through any particular person's mind and consciousness at any given moment should be enough to make us stop short in wonder.

Some scientists call this process of emergence producing "something else from nothing but", and these phenomena can include everything from intangible tools to concrete systems properties—anything that helps a complex system adapt and innovate, become more than it was, and do more than would have been possible relying only on the elements of its physical system. Emergent phenomena are usually not ephemeral, and once a complex adaptive system generates one, there is no unwinding the process. (On the other hand, emergent *properties,* such as the wetness or hardness of materials produced in molecular systems, are often ephemeral, or at least subject to "phase transitions".) In fact, probably the most important aspect of emergence is how it creates an added level of organization within a given system and allows for the (top down) alteration of such system's structural dynamics, often adaptive benefit.

This is particularly true in the human brain system. Most aspects of mind, such as consciousness and a sense of agency in the world, having emerged from the complex mechanics of the human brain system, create new (and permanent) organizational levels within the system's hierarchy. For example, emotions emerge to motivate our brains and bodies to move and accomplish certain important feats. Fear and anger help us survive, love prompts us to procreate, and other primary emotions generate feelings that drive sophisticated social strategies, which also factor into our capacity to thrive and survive. Emotions like disgust may have originally emerged to help us avoid potentially poisonous plants and foods, but eventually they led to the emergence of not just disgust but other more nuanced *feelings* about other people's behaviors, which help us avoid getting mixed up with those who might threaten our ability to thrive in different social contexts. The list of emergent emotions, feelings, motivations, desires, thoughts, etc. that drive the functioning of our brain and bodies, even define our personhood, is long and very relevant to the whole concept of networked thinking.

Emergent emotions, feelings, and other aspects of mind can be manipulated, by engaging in various mental disciplines such as trained meditation practices, but they cannot be destroyed, as long as the brain systems that gave rise to such phenomena are active, healthy, and in balance. Similarly, in other complex adaptive systems, such as an economic market, as phenomena like consumer demand emerge, they will remain in place until the system itself is destroyed. (Moreover, such phenomena continue to become more complex themselves, as in the case of market demand becoming increasingly segmented according to distinct demographics, preferences, and similar factors that make each consumer unique.)

Because the whole concept of emergence in complex adaptive systems is an elusive one, it is difficult to make a hard and fast science of it. Emergent phenomena are themselves not easy to identify, describe, and catalogue. Even more problematic is the task of analyzing the dynamics by which such emergent phenomena operate in cause and effect with the components of the systems from which they are generated. Does our consciousness of something, our desire or will for an event to happen, or our gathered feelings about someone affect what happens the next moment in our brain systems, or does some ingrained combination of neural firings and systems outputs determine what emerges in our minds and consciousness? Are the premonitions we have and the ideas that pop into our minds caused by specific sets of dynamics in our brain systems? Nobody has the definitive answers to these questions and thousands of others like them, but we do know that some emergent phenomena can cause different effects on the underlying systems that generate them. (More on this later.)

We also know that we experience the world around us using this emergent phenomena called "mind" and that it serves us well as a kind of mental space, which we might use to sort out our thoughts and feelings, make various predictions or calculations about what we should do next, and focus our attention on what actually is taking place around us. Moreover, the emergent mind allows for the development of mental tools, some of which are now essential for human survival in the complex world we now inhabit. For example, written language allowed our minds to acquire the important social tools of logic and reason, which improve our communication with each other. Similarly, the invention of the telegraph made it possible for us to enhance our capacities for Theory of Mind and grasp how other people were having simultaneous experiences. (The advent of the telephone, then TV, the personal computer, 24 Hour International News, and the Internet/Web extended even further our appreciation of how others think and behave, in contrast to our thoughts and feelings.)

Maybe the most intriguing aspect of our emergent mind is how it operates in a very complex cause and effect relationship with the many systems of our brains and within the overall constraints of the whole integrated brain system. Independent as it may seem to us at times, the emergent human mind remains to some extent tethered to the human brain system that generates it, and if that system is frozen in panic, or addled by narcotics, the mind is constrained by those effects. Sometimes these experienced constraints of mind seem temporary and trivial, as when we feel mentally slow under the influences of the flu, and sometimes they are far more permanent and restrictive. For example, physical constraints of our underlying brain systems are basically the reason why our minds cannot visualize more than three dimensional space, owing to the limitations of the brain's visual processing and object representation systems.

The science of emergence is clear on one thing—some phenomena and systems properties cause effects within their underlying systems, and some do not. "Strong" emergent phenomena are able to exert top down adaptive influences on the system that generates them. Human brain systems create aspects of mind such as self-reflective consciousness so that a sense of identity and agency can emerge, within a concept of personhood, in order to generate the idea of "personal responsibility" and create beings who seek intelligence and desire to engage in purposeful activity, all of which enhances the chances of survival. Are not people who are motivated by some emergent sense of personal responsibility or purpose inclined to think and act more collaboratively than those who are not? In short, however it came to be this way, human brain systems are currently wired to necessarily generate aspects of mind that make us want to become more effective agents of change on a whole range of matters, whether that means expanding our collective intelligence or treating each other more thoughtfully.

Mind and will

The centuries of philosophical debate since Descartes notwithstanding, there can no longer be any question that certain aspects of mind emerge from the self-organizing processes of the human brain system. The previously referred to research on Split-Brain patients is proof of this. For purposes of this book and our investigation of the dynamics of the human brain system and its capacity for networked thinking, it may be important to make the distinctions between not only strong and weak emergent phenomena but also the properties of our conscious and unconscious minds. The human brain system processes tremendous amounts of information every millisecond, but very little of it is able to be processed in Working Memory, where it would be available for conscious manipulation. As beings with a strong sense of emergent agency, we often forget that many of our thoughts and behaviors are in fact driven by what we are not consciously aware of or even think we might desire. The great majority of our acts are in fact programmed by brain systems that give rise to automatic and other unconscious thoughts and behaviors, which are not easy for our minds to control or direct.

Several decades ago, neuroscientist Benjamin Libet famously offered up an experiment that tried to explain these elusive emergent phenomena of conscious will and behavior. The experiment involved measuring the time frame when a subject pushed a bottom, compared to the timeframe when the "signal" was transmitted to the sensorimotor cortex and the timeframe in which the subject reported forming his intent to push the button. The results indicated that the signal occurred before the reported intent was formed. In terms of not just neuroscience but brain systems science, there are a number of possible explanations for these results, but Libet originally concluded that what we might sense is the "free" will to act as we please may instead be a phenomenon that emerges within our conscious minds, *after the fact,* so as to generate within our minds a sense of agency that is critical to our ability to motivate ourselves and insure our survival.

Other similar experiments have been undertaken recently, without providing any more insight into the interplay between the experience of conscious choice and the timing of commands generated within the brain, and the whole concept of emergent will—when and how it is freely exercised and what effects it might be able to cause on the brain system from which it emerges—continues to be widely debated. A great number of neuroscientists and philosophers have countered Libet's conclusions, stating that the results of his experiment only speak to a very limited subset of human activities, like pushing a button, and that the more complex the action or longer the time frame involved, the greater will be our opportunity to exercise free will.

Personally, I find Libet's conclusions not only reassuring but helpful to our deeper understanding of emergent phenomena in the human person. Just the other day, I was driving down the right side of a four lane urban street and pulled into a left hand turn lane, then started into my turn when the green arrow appeared on the stop light. A split second later, I slammed on the brakes, as a car from the outer lane of oncoming traffic raced through what I must assume was a red light, unless it was malfunctioning. (I did wonder, because after I collected myself, looked up at the light to make sure that I did in fact have a green turn arrow, and began once again to make my left hand turn, another car zoomed right by my front bumper!) In any event, as I analyzed the whole situation after the fact, I realized that I had started to hit the brakes well before I fully understood what was going on or had a chance to choose a defensive strategy.

A very fast-acting circuit operating outside my consciousness had sent a command—and one I am very grateful for—to my sensorimotor systems well before I could possibly have consciously made a decision about what to do.

Later in the day, I recalled another incident over 30 years ago in which I was approaching an urban intersection when my peripheral vision picked up a car coming from my left (and which I later realized my brain had immediately intuited was not slowing down). Sure enough, the car barreled through a red light and into the intersection just as my car entered it, and if I had had time to think about things, I would have slammed on the brakes, but for reasons that only my fast-acting subcortical brain and unconscious mind understood, I found myself jamming down the accelerator instead, managing to race through the intersection just ahead of the other car, miraculously avoiding a collision. So it seems clear to me that sometimes our brain systems would not be able to act fast enough to save us from physical disaster if they had to wait for conscious processing and willful behavior to kick in all the time—in other words, sometimes the exercise of "free" will would not be optimal, and our brain systems are geared to save us from that option. There are times for the exercise of "free" will and times to simply react, without will at all. The key factor is our awareness—awareness of how our brain systems work and when we have an opportunity to control them, using the wondrous faculties of our emergent minds.

Certainly, there are plenty of situations we are confronted with in life that require us to gather information and feedback over extended periods of time, not just in the course of a few seconds or minutes. Life changing decisions and actions require that we take the time to seek out diversity of input and perspective, even engage in some trial and error feedback. For example, it might be a good idea to experiment with a few different jobs before making a career choice, or date various types of people before deciding on a marriage partner. These are not the kind of decisions that Libet and others have experimented with, and it seems unlikely that studies like Libet's could even be designed to work on such long-term, life changing decision-making processes.

That said, and given that the complex adaptive human brain system's structural dynamics are both non-linear and hierarchical, there is every reason to believe that free will and open-ended choice in life are critical components of the human mind. Hierarchical structures necessarily generate prioritization, so if human brain systems provide the mind with the ability to prioritize some of the brain's needs and strategies, it seems likely that the mind would also be able to prioritize its own set of thoughts, desires, strategies, and needs. And if the mind can prioritize its own interests and goals, it must by definition be able to freely choose which ones to pursue. And that is my definition of free will, regardless of what Libet's experiment might suggest about the mechanics of decision making in human brain systems. Moreover, whatever else can be said about the human mind, it is aware of its own existence and agency power, not only to choose what it will focus on but what it intends the brain and body to do in executing its plans. So perhaps the whole issue is not very complicated after all and can be neatly resolved by stating that if the human mind is the strong emergent phenomenon we know it to be, then by definition we have *some* form of free will.

Consciousness

As with the non-linear, hierarchical dynamics of human brain systems and the emergence of will and choice, so also with the emergent phenomenon of consciousness. Without consciousness, mind and will lose their meaning. However they emerge within our minds, purpose and meaning are essential to our mental well-being, and consciousness is a central factor in our entire approach to life. Consciousness relies on attention to stimuli created by key soma-sensory brain systems, together with healthy memory systems, to generate a fundamental awareness of self, the capacity for introspection, and the ability to access mental states. It represents the fundamental function that gives rise to human planning and decision making. It more or less defines our species.

While the nature and source of human consciousness has been debated by philosophers and scientists for centuries, only in the last few decades has it really been doggedly pursued by neuroscientists. As one would expect, there are a wide variety of views on the subject, many of which I sought to summarize in a White Paper I wrote a few years ago. Nevertheless, it is possible to identify a few key points on the dynamics of human consciousness.

First, we are able to make some observations about what is entailed in certain aspects of human consciousness, particularly metacognition and self-reflection. As far as we know, humans are the only beings who are aware of their own awareness, capacities, and mortality. Provided our thoughts come into consciousness (which obviously does not happen all the time), we can know that we do think and that thinking directs a great deal of our consciousness. We now even know that our thinking affects what goes on in our brains, hearts, and other organs in our bodies. Equally importantly, we are aware that we think self-reflectively—we can imagine and predict the results of our thoughts and behaviors, assess the value or successfulness of them in achieving our intended goals, and decide to make adjustments to those behaviors. We can make observations not only about others' consciousness but our own as well, and in this capacity, we are essentially able to have virtually simultaneous subjective and objective experiences of ourselves and others. Consciousness allows us introspective access to our various mental states—not just thinking, but perceiving, feeling, and emoting as well—so that we might make, and continue to update, strategies for our own survival.

Second, over the last few decades, we have come to understand the many possible explanations of and for consciousness, even if we find it hard to define the phenomenon clearly. Theories about the source of human consciousness range from the synchronization of electromagnetic waves across the entire brain at 40 Hz (Hameroff) to the integration of various brain systems signals in a particular region of the brain, such as the claustrum. (Crick and Koch) In my White Paper, I tried to present a synthesis of the many different perspectives offered by various scientists and philosophers, but for my money, the most succinct and viable single explanation comes from neuroscientist Antonio Demasio. (I am not addressing here the type of consciousness that Eastern philosophers refer to as a phenomenon that may hold the universe's self-organizing intelligence, what might be called "Universal" or "Collective" Consciousness.)

Damasio describes consciousness in escalating levels of systems organization (and self-awareness), from the "Protoself" to "Core Consciousness" to "Extended Consciousness". Each aspect, or level, of consciousness is generated from the "bottom up" and relies on the level beneath it in order to manifest. Beginning with the Protoself, a phenomenon that Damasio claims exists within all animals and emerges in humans from the workings of the brain stem and closely surrounding networks, human consciousness begins with a sentience of being alive in the world and extends into the core consciousness of emotion, sensorimotor processing, and all the way up to self-reflective recognition of subjective experience. While Damasio's Protoself and Core Consciousness includes the subjective appreciation of what emotions and feelings one is able to experience, the phenomenon of Extended Consciousness requires the introduction of sophisticated memory systems and the ability to recall one's own subjective and objective history of experience. Consciousness of who we are and what might come next requires that we remember who we have been and what we have done already. Sadly, the consciousness of someone suffering from Alzheimer's would lack that critical component.

This approach seems to me to fit ideally with the fundamental non-linear and hierarchical nature of the human complex adaptive brain system, as discussed above. Moreover, it depicts both a nature and source of human consciousness that is consistent with our self-reported observations of subjective experiences in life. The capacities of the human mind, and perhaps even the many characteristics of human intelligence, all begin with awareness, and it seems that consciousness should possess parallel characteristics. Nothing happens in the mind, or consciousness, until we come awake and are aware of where we are, who we have been, how we got there, what has happened so far in our lives, what seems to be about to happen next, and so on. Once awake and aware of our surroundings, we have the ability to focus our minds and consciousness on what emotions we are experiencing, what thoughts and feelings are coursing through our minds, and what we might need to do, in the short-term or long-term, to enhance our chances of achieving specific goals. Clearly, each of these processes involves some type or level of awareness.

In fact, for purposes of this book and our full appreciation of how to extend human intelligence or shift our individual and collective human consciousness by using networked thinking, it may be far more important to focus on the subject of awareness than any larger concept of consciousness, as described above. Perhaps it is the simple awareness that we have minds and choices about what thoughts, feelings, attitudes, and perspectives we will adopt that matters more in our decision making than any other aspect of mind. Interestingly, in recent studies, the capacity for becoming aware—of one's mind, emotions, social intelligence, and ability to make choices—proved to be more critical to good decision making than either raw (IQ type) intelligence or experience.

Ego

One other emergent phenomenon of the complex adaptive human brain system bears mentioning in this book. Made popular by Freud and decades of psychologists who followed, the human ego has an undeniable impact on human behavior, thinking, intelligence, and decision making. Simple awareness of the ego as an emergent phenomenon and its resultant characteristics will make the difference between being ruled by reactive behaviors and engaging in mindful decision making. For the last several decades, it has become popular to talk about emotional and social intelligence, but the truth is that self-mastery and intelligent decision making starts with the simple awareness that the phenomenon we refer to as the "ego" is "strongly" emergent and that its definable characteristics and tendencies therefore generate significant influences on the workings of our minds and the operations of our brain systems.

As discussed in the next chapter, the brain relies heavily for its cognitive processing on two significant systems—Default and Integrated—each of which produces highly self-referential systems dynamics that probably serve as the source of our emergent egos. It also seems possible that the human mind creates the ego as the "agent" primarily responsible for conceiving of and driving appropriate strategies and measures of self-protection, especially the ones that develop our tools and assets as "social animals". Once this "agent" emerges within the human mind, it is able to generate its own emergent properties, including the social and emotional defensive instincts we develop over time, which help spur us on in pursuit of work and survival.

Ironically, it is the emergent ego that seems to fill our minds with the many thoughts and feelings of inadequacy, fear, defensiveness, and what not, which invariably interfere with thoughtful analysis and intelligent decision making. Thoughts and feelings that seem to be generated by the ego can virtually shut down higher level thinking, turn us into bumbling idiots for some period of time, and make us do things that we sorely regret when we do have a chance to think about them. Becoming aware of the ego's emergent characteristics and origins diffuses some of its effect, but as an emergent phenomenon, the ego is never going to disappear—nor should it, for the very same reasons that some or our behaviors lack free will, as mentioned above. On the other hand, we must also be clear that engaging in networked thinking is impossible if the emergent ego is *controlling* our minds and thoughts.

7

ORGANIZATIONAL STRUCTURE AND KEY FUNCTIONAL SYSTEMS OF THE HUMAN BRAIN SYSTEM

Understanding the value and mechanics of networked thinking requires that we understand the fundamental cognitive systems that drive much of what happens in the emergent mind. We need to grasp how neural networks, circuits, and systems in the human brain are networked together to build a hierarchical organizational structure of increasingly complex systems and "higher" functions, from the bottom up. But we also must factor in how such a hierarchical organizational structure influences the mechanics and functions of all brain systems, from the top down.

Ultimately, the dynamics of human thinking functionally tied to this hierarchical organizational structure. Human brain systems that give rise to sensory perception, working memory, and other cognitive functions lay the foundation for our ability to think. Thinking is a prerequisite to decision making, and decision making is essential to survival. What becomes particularly significant about the emergence of human thinking, however, is that at each successive organizational level within the human brain/ mind, it becomes more difficult to predict what will happen, yet ironically what happens at each level becomes increasingly important in terms of the effects it has at lower organizational levels. In others words, while it might be simple for neuroscientists to predict what will happen as the human brain system processes certain information, it would be much more difficult to determine how that processing manifests as content of the mind and virtually impossible to anticipate what thoughts might then be engendered in the mind. And yet, we also know from countless studies and brain scans that thoughts directly affect the overall content of the mind and are able to direct what happens in many different information processing activities of the human brain system.

We can look at EEG, fMRI or PET scans and reasonably predict what functions or behaviors attach to many identifiable regions of the brain, but we cannot easily predict what characteristics of mind or elements of thought or feeling will emerge from the activation of such functional areas. Conversely, neuroscientists are now able to use certain tools, from EEG outputs to optogenetic mechanisms, to track how thoughts appear to direct certain sensorimotor information processing activities in the brain. Of course, within the ever-changing, even somewhat stochastic nature of the human brain system, these processes are to some extent always working simultaneously in both directions, from the top down and bottom up, which is precisely what one would expect of a truly complex *adaptive* system like the human brain.

There is more to this bottom up/top down set of adaptive dynamics than that, however. Thoughts are fleeting and concentrated, extended thinking is difficult to sustain. The same is often true of the mind, which is easily distracted and requires considerable energy to maintain its focus. Changes in thinking and content of mind are natural and regular, but this is less true of the underlying brain system itself—although the human brain system is highly dynamic and plastic, it is primarily quite static and predictable in its general operations. Remember, it has a lot to do and changing structure demands valuable energy.

On the other hand, while the human brain system is indeed more predictable than the workings of the human mind and the emergence of human thought, when its organizational structure is altered, the resulting changes ripple out into mind and thinking with considerable leverage. For example, look at what a tremendous difference it makes whether a person's memory system has been stressed by a great number of traumatic events (does not even have to involve PTSD). If such a person's brain system encounters stimuli that immediately tap into such memories and elicit strong, associated emotional reactions, that person's mind is hardly at ease, free to generate all sorts of creative thoughts. The good news is that this leverage works both ways, and we can indeed chose to think in ways that condition our minds and promote the use of brain systems that do lead to open and creative thinking.

In this last chapter of Part II, I will describe what I deem to be the key functional brain systems that: 1) give rise to distinct emergent mindsets, which in turn drive certain types of thinking, and 2) influence, if not dictate, the types of information networks that self-organize within the human brain system and continue to evolve, based on the thinking they help to generate.

The two primary cognitive systems of the complex adaptive human brain

In the diagram below, I have sought to capture, in the form of a matrix that highlights key systems and network dynamics, some of the significant components of the human brain's two primary cognitive systems, which I have labelled "Default" and "Integrated". I chose to include within this matrix the known characteristics of the human brain system's right and left hemispheres for two reasons: 1) to highlight how the human brain system's information networks are designed to build in both redundancy and leverage (most functional systems exist in both hemispheres, but there are unique characteristics in each), and 2) to emphasize how different brain systems generate discrete forms of emergent minds, or mindsets. (Split-Brain research performed over the last 50 years by neuroscientists like Roger Sperry and Michael Gazzaniga make it clear that each hemisphere is able to independently generate a "conscious" mind that can "interpret" and make sense of what is going on, regardless of what might actually be taking place within the underlying brain systems that the patient does not have conscious access to. Moreover, other evidence, such as the post-stroke testimony of Dr. Jill Bolte Taylor, herself a neuroscientist, makes it clear that these "hemisphere oriented minds" are different in nature and capability from the emergent mind that is generated from a completely integrated, healthy, and fully functional human brain system.)

	DEFAULT SYSTEM	INTEGRATED SYSTEM
Left hemisphere	Concrete, sensory processing; object identification and association; data and information pattern analysis; analytical, linear thinking, linear cause and effect focus; literal language orientation, compartmentalized perspective; fixed mindset, beliefs; fear, reward driven orientation; limited global awareness and consciousness; illusory "self"; emergent ego, will, intent, motivation, collaboration; focus on past	Integration of internal and external perceived "realities" within the brain (e.g. limbic system, social brain, anticipating consequences of actions, executive judgment and choice, nuanced thinking); growth mindset; prediction from Bayesian inference, non-linear cause and effect; cross-disciplinary decision making; integration of brain/body; complex thoughts; focus on future; emergent phenomena of morality, reciprocity, altruism
Right hemisphere	Coherent ideas, beliefs, "truths", worldviews, based on "external realities"; multiple cause and effect possibilities; prediction based on statistical analysis; mechanical feedforward and feedback systems to regulate thought, gain balance, maintain social status/position; emotional evaluation and reconciliation of emotionally charged memories;	Dynamic, holistic , strategic thinking; embracing failure; thinking "outside the box"; mindful perception of reality and risk taking; integration of complex emergent phenomena such as soul, body/mind, brain/mind, existential choice, holographic self and universe; awareness of collective consciousness; courage and perseverance, hope, faith; imagination; empathy, compassion, love; other orientation, metaphysical reward focus

MATRIX OF HUMAN BRAIN STRUCTURES/SYSTEMS RELEVANT TO ORGANIZATIONAL AND CONSUMER BEHAVIOR
- **Default system**: brain stem, cerebellum, limbic system (basal ganglia, amygdala, hypothalamus, hippocampus, thalamus), sensory-motor processing system, thalamocoritcal nuclei, OIO system, posterior cingulate cortex (PCC), nucleus accumbens, lateral habenula; ganglia, anterior cingulate cortex (ACC)
- **Integrated system**: Default system components, claustrum, insula, anterior cingulate gyrus, pre-frontal cortex

Default System

The primary functional tool the human brain system uses to process *adaptive* information involves a very sophisticated system for identifying, representing, cataloguing, and comparing "objects"—what I call the "Object Identification and Orientation" ("OIO") system. As suggested in Figure 4 and discussed in greater detail below, the human brain system treats everything as an "object", so the OIO system processes information on "objects" from both the "outside world" and the "inside world". Accordingly, the OIO system comprises all of the systems that process sensory stimuli, laying the foundation for "identifying" the things that our minds conceive of as the physical objects that make up our external reality and which must be navigated and otherwise dealt with in order to insure our survival. Together with what I call the "Self-referential" system ("S/R"), which appears to be centered in the posterior cingulate cortex ("PCC"), the OIO system represents two foundational components of what I will refer to throughout this book as the "Default system".

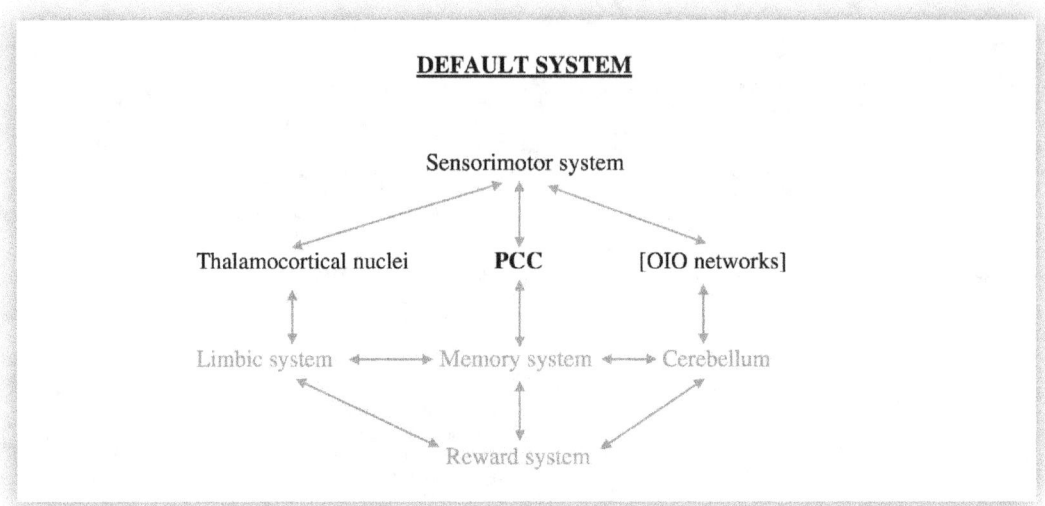

The Default system is just that—the system our brain normally defaults to, for several reasons: 1) it is accorded a priority position in the hierarchy of the brain's information processing systems (including the delivery of energy to do that processing), because of its obvious role in survival based goals and mechanisms, 2) it encompasses the most fundamental of cognitive chores, particularly the processing of sensory stimuli that carries with it any new and relevant information from the external environment, and 3) it manages the process of cataloguing information bits and patterns into "objects", a prerequisite to navigating one's physical environment.

Given the mechanics of the OIO system and how much it factors into the dynamics of the larger Default system, it is critical to understand that to the human brain system everything is an "object"—not just physical objects, but data, information sets, symbols, ideas, concepts—everything that might be relevant to any of its functions. Equally importantly, the human brain essentially generates internal *representations* of these "objects" so that it can compare, contrast, and associates these "objects" toward the end of: 1) creating a baseline "external reality", in order to allow for efficient navigation of its environment, for purposes ranging from the simple gathering of food, in the early days of our species' existence, to the now complex implications of maintaining one's social status, a prerequisite to survival in the modern world; 2) making distinctions about "objects" in the brain's environment, as internally represented, so as to continually update its "knowledge bases" and capacity for making predictions that enhance its chances of survival.

These "objects" are likely encoded into dynamic neural networks, by the neural interconnections that are formed and the speed at which such networks "fire". Jeff Hawkins might well be describing the precise mechanics of how "objects" are recorded within the OIO system in what he calls "Sparse Distributed Representations" ("SDR's"), which he characterizes as three dimensional neural networks that use three or more "layers" of the six-layered cortex. His theory is that three dimensional networks can form and reform into exponentially large numbers of network *states*, each one of which can represent a data set that seemingly could be "chunked" to reflect a specific "object", and "rechunked" to reflect countless derivatives of that "object" as well.

Using this type of system, the brain could then manipulate these complex neural links and synaptic firing speeds in order to: 1) identify, represent, and catalogue every "object" that is either "perceived" by the brain or generated within the mind, 2) distinguish, contrast, and compare any "object", and 3) make both simple and complex associations among different "objects". Let us be clear on what actually happens in the human brain system when it contrasts, compares, and associates "objects".

As we know, our brain systems are basically prediction machines, which hunger for new and relevant information in order to keep making good, situation appropriate predictions. In a process known as "Bayesian updating", the human brain system also continues to process different information patterns, tries to make increasingly better predictions, and *discards the information that has proven not to help any given prediction*. So for example, over time, your brain system begins to process patterns of information surrounding cloud formation and color in order to predict when it might rain. If you move to a place with different weather patterns, your brain system will use Bayesian updating techniques to adjust those predictions, based on new and relevant information about cloud patterns, how fast the weather changes, etc. By the same token, your brain system would also begin to eliminate patterns of information that did not appear relevant to rainy weather patterns in your new environment.

And when it comes to comparing, contrasting, and associating "objects", the process is basically the same. Your brain system identifies patterns of cloud formation, predicts rain, then based on past experiences, also predicts that the rain (as "object") will make you wet ("object"), that being wet usually makes you feel cold and uncomfortable ("object"), and that if you don proper rain gear ("object"), becoming uncomfortably wet can be prevented. Thus, your brain's Default system is using these predictive algorithms to essentially compare and contrast the "object" of feeling wet and cold to the "object" of a dry and warm state, then associates the "object" of rain with an "object" such as a rain coat or umbrella that, based on experience, it predicts will keep you dry. So, in essence, all of the human brain system's algorithms for comparing, contrasting, and associating "objects" are simply predictions that are made by sorting through information deemed either relevant or irrelevant to those predictions.

Another way of looking at this phenomenon is through the lens of Information Theory. Brain systems that have processed lots of information are adept at identifying the relevant messages required to make accurate predictions, while segregating out all of the irrelevant noise. (Given the dynamics of this OIO system, when the human brain system does encounter new or unexpected relevant information, different bio-chemical signals—notably in the form of dopamine neurotransmitters—are released to make sure the brain system pays special attention.)

Viewing the predictive mechanisms and decision-making processes of the human brain system in this way can help us design and operate more effective Knowledge Networks as well. Sometimes the most strategic decision is to refrain from doing something, in which case it is critical to know what will not work, and that can only be sorted out by brains that have a lot of experience in discarding irrelevant information. As discussed in Chapter Nine, the beauty of Knowledge Networks is that this expertise can be developed within the individual decision maker's brain system, as well as in the "collective brain system" of the entire Knowledge Network.

The information processing mechanics of the Default system make it possible for the brain to keep "chunking" and "rechunking" data and information patterns to form increasingly complex forms of "objects" (e.g., moving from the concrete to the theoretical). And this is precisely how the emergent mind manipulates "objects" to construct mental models and "think" about them. Although no one really knows how the brain creates the mind's capacity to "think", I maintain that thinking is simply a very sophisticated emergent property of the brain/mind's capacity to identify, catalogue, and manipulate "objects", in a host of different ways, leading to "forms" of thinking, such as what we might call linear, circular, rational, or hypothetical.

The human brain system could use a particular neural network of SDRs to represent the "object" of a simple system, replete with some of its key characteristics, such as linear cause and effect dynamics. The brain/mind would then use the "object" as a placeholder for the concept of a system, so that it could later distinguish it from other "objects" that exhibit cause and effect characteristics but are not simple systems (e.g., the linear effect of a falling rock caused by gravitational force, which is part of a very complex system). Similarly, the brain could create many other SDRs to represent all the simple systems that the mind would eventually need to catalogue as "objects" in order to compare them and "think" about what to do about them. For example, the simple chemical system that changes the state of water to solid or gas under certain atmospheric and temperature conditions also generates phase transitions in other compounds too, but usually under different conditions; the human brain system is able to catalogue different kinds of liquids as distinct "objects", which allows the human mind to make important associations regarding these "objects" and engenders in those minds the kind of thinking that prompts us, for example, to put alcohol based coolants rather than water in our modern vehicles' radiators.

Complex thinking occurs when the human brain system continues to rechunk pieces of information into increasingly complex sets of SDRs, representing increasingly complex "objects". The brain/mind can then easily compare, distinguish, and make relevant associations between and among these complex "objects", which constitutes the essence of complex thinking. By the same token, the human brain system can also use these same mechanics to transform complex representations and symbols of "objects" into simpler ones, which is basically what happens in synthesized thinking. (This brings to mind the notion that notion that genius is the art of rendering the complex simple.) So for example, instead of trying to describe the complexity of various fan behaviors in the sports world, in order to analyze the sources and meanings of such behaviors, the human brain system can distill the entire range of observed behaviors into one simple concept—fanaticism—which itself becomes an "object" that is represented neuro-physiologically in the brain by a single SDR. The brain/mind can then manipulate this "object" to do all sorts of sophisticated thinking about why otherwise sane people become insane over their sports teams. Interestingly, the way in which the OIO represents and associates

101

"objects" is probably why our minds like analogies and metaphors so much when they are trying to grasp a novel concept or idea.

The mechanics of the OIO system are fundamental to human thinking. While other primates can identify, catalogue, and associate "objects", then represent them as "symbols" that can be further manipulated in their brain systems and mental workspaces (in some form of "mind"), our capacity for language provides us with more sophisticated symbols, which we are able to manipulate in order to "think". It is quite possible that the dynamic remodeling of three dimensional networks in our brains, the constant chunking and rechunking of data, and the consequent capacity of our minds to manipulate patterns of information is precisely what makes humans the amazing thinking machines, creative decision makers, and strategic planners that we have become (at least most of the time!).

Unfortunately, this OIO system is also the component of the Default system that can most effectively compromise our thinking as well. To begin with, what if our brains do a poor job of identifying, representing, and cataloguing an "object" in the first place? The OIO system of someone who has never seen or been told about a zebra might catalogue the "object" as a horse. Ensuing comparisons and associations of that "horse's" behavior to real horses could lead to error and confused thinking, just as is true if one finds that the original premise of a particular theory or argument is false. The problem would be compounded when we get into increasingly significant and nuanced "objects". For example, what if a central bank chief's brain identifies and catalogues a temporary downturn as a recession? The "object" that is a "recession" will engender in the brains of all the central bank decision makers different comparisons and associations than would the "object" of a downturn, particularly with respect to key "objects" like unemployment and money supply figures, all of which would completely alter the thinking of the central bank decision makers.

For most of us, in our daily lives, this issue is much simpler, but no less exigent, than thinking about and making decisions on economic policy. And yet, day in and day out, we find ourselves either not thinking very much or not thinking very effectively. The major source of this problem is really quite straightforward in my view—so much our thinking goes wrong simply because we allow it to be governed by the Default system mechanics of sloppy, careless, lazy, or even innocently misguided identification and representation of "objects", ranging from another person's feelings to what is healthy food and behavior. Our thinking would be much clearer and more effective: if we consistently stopped to listen and observe, allow our brain systems to accurately identify and catalogue the "object" of a colleague's emotion as "frustration" rather than "anger"; if we took the time to read the information on what food is good for the human body and allow our brain systems to properly identify and catalogue those "objects", then associate them with appropriate behavior "objects"; if we disciplined our brain systems to make distinctions between the "objects" of "self-esteem" and "pride", so that they could be properly catalogued in our brain systems and ultimately our minds could think clearly about the associated behaviors that should accompany each one...the list goes on and on.

In fact, after laziness and carelessness, the second biggest issue generated within the Default system's OIO system seems to be the challenges it faces in distinguishing, comparing, and associating "objects". Assuming we have woken to the task and our brain systems are not overcome by some form of inertia, there is probably no more consistent and serious threat to effective human thinking than the failure to make proper distinctions. "Mistakes" are not the same thing as "errors"; disapproving of a person is not the same thing as decrying that person's behavior; socialism is not the same thing as communism; sadness is not the same as depression; achievement is not the same as success; and so on and so forth. In the fast-acting, often unconscious trance of Default system processing, the human brain fails to make key distinctions, particularly in "objects" with complex information patterns. As noted earlier, our brain systems simply have much to do and not enough processing power to consistently and accurately identify and catalogue all the "objects" it encounters, every second, so it takes great discipline to direct the work of our brain systems in making proper distinctions. This is precisely where our strongly emergent minds can be most effective, asserting their top down influence (in a process we call "mindfulness") to focus our brain systems on the differences in information patterns that define distinct "objects" and catalogue them accurately. This type of disciplined mindfulness starts with the awareness of how the OIO system works and how predisposed our brain systems are to be governed by the Default system.

The Default system also warps our thinking by the countless unwarranted associations between "objects" that are generated from within the OIO system. Without our reactive, fast-acting Default systems, would we really associate certain races (as "objects") with pejorative characteristics like ignorance, sloth, and avarice (also as "objects")? Would we all flunk the Harvard Implicit Association test, just as Malcolm Gladwell did, notwithstanding his determination not to do so and the conscious sensibilities he must carry with him, being himself of mixed racial descent? Even the "innocent" associations the OIO system makes between "objects" like a certain look on another person's face and the conclusion that such person is uneasy about something can lead to a false prediction that he or she is lying. Misguided assessments of information patterns, rapid and poor predictions of what those patterns mean, and failure to *re*assess what the Default system generates as outputs contribute heavily to the unfortunate and often misguided associations our brain systems make between "objects" and which results so often in ineffective thinking.

Interestingly, this might be one of the domains where machines actually do a better job than humans. The various computational methods and tools the Default system uses to make all these "object" comparisons and associations revolve around statistical mechanics and Boolean logic, the same tools used in software programs and computational algorithms. Boolean logic is familiar to almost everyone these days, because it is what the search engines use to comb the Web for queried information, using the four basic commands of "AND", "OR", "COPY", and "NOT". Statistical mechanics involves a particular linear approach to measuring changing probabilities, which the Default system uses to make its never-ending series of predictions. Accordingly, it would seem that the Default system operates more like a Turing computer than the Integrated system does, but the truth is that its calculations are sometimes high-jacked by other factors, like emotion, while machines are not. (The Integrated system operates more like an analog parallel information processor than the Default system does and is able to integrate more sophisticated tools like Bayesian inference and genetic algorithms into its predictive mechanisms.)

Finally, for the reasons discussed below, the Default system's operational networks, circuits, and subsystems tend to be more recursive than they are in many of the pre-frontal systems that are important components of the Integrated system. Highly recursive networks and systems generate stronger than normal reinforcing influences, so the emotions and thoughts that are processed in the Default system are more apt to get stuck in closed loop repetition than would occur within the Integrated system. I expect that when we get songs "stuck in our heads" or find it difficult to let go of a particular thought or emotion, the mechanics of the Default system are to blame. Of course, this whole process becomes even more insidious and potentially destructive to our thinking when other influences, such as those of the S/R system, combine to make these recurring emotions and thoughts feel particularly personal. There is little that emerges within the human mind that is more debilitating than thinking that is entirely self-focused, particularly when it is also self-destructive or counterproductive.

Despite its potential inhibiting aspects, the S/R system is central to human survival. Within the Default system, the OIO system interoperates with the S/R system to make it possible for our minds to achieve the physical, mental, and emotional orientation that is essential to: 1) generating an internal sense of "self" and state of equilibrium, 2) creating within the mind a sense that such "self" possesses the capacity for agency in the world, and 3) orienting the Default system toward adopting perceptions, strategies, and behaviors designed first and foremost to preserve that "self". Given the powerful nature of these functions, it is easy to see how the human mind orients toward the "self" when the Default system is dominant. Once again, it is simply a matter of being aware of the Default system's components and operational dynamics, so as to understand both their benefits and potential dangers.

The PCC (posterior cingulate cortex), which as its name suggests is located near the mid-brain and toward the "posterior" of the brain, seems to act as the key network node within the S/R system, together with the cerebellum. It seems that the PCC may be the system that is responsible for taking the output of the OIO, comparing, associating, and contrasting "objects" in the context of perceived environmental conditions, and generating assessments about what is going on at any given moment. In addition, thalamocortical nuclei, and other networks that create feedforward and feedback systems within the Default system, may effectively connect up the OIO system to the limbic system and the PCC.

This close interconnection of the OIO system, PCC, and limbic system presents several potential issues. First, because of its proximity to the PCC, the limbic system can easily insinuate emotions into an otherwise objective assessment of what is going on and create a whole raft of emotion laden "judgments" rather than objective assessments. Second, because the Default system uses predictive models that rely on extrapolations from the past, it is prone to producing negative self-talk. The OIO system generates the easy comparisons between the "objects" of our own careers, marriages, bank accounts, friends and what not, then the PCC turns those comparisons into self-referential judgments. That often leads to other pejorative associations, which can soon be followed by thoughts that whatever has happened in the past will define the way it unfolds in the future. The Default system can quickly generate cycles involving a wide range of thought and feeling, which means that negative self-talk can spiral easily down into irrationality.

As noted in Figure 5, the Default system depends on various feedback systems in the OIO and cerebellum that help orient the whole body in time and space, as well as control motor functions. Furthermore, recent discoveries of "place cells" in the hippocampus by neuroscientist John O'Keefe seems to suggest that in addition to being a central factor in human memory systems, the hippocampus is a critical part of the brain's "orientation" system as well, encoding "objects" and patterns of "objects" that represent "locations" in time and space that are essential to our physical and mental mobility. Additionally, research by O'Keefe's students Edvard Moser and May-Britt Moser on "grid cells" in the entorhinal cortex, adjacent to the hippocampus, supports the notion that both these areas may be part of a larger navigational system embedded in the Default system.

The central role that is apparently played by the hippocampus and the rest of the limbic system in the operational dynamics of the Default system is one of the factors that gives it so much power and control. Because it deals with important survival based emotions such as fear, the limbic system has developed a priority position in the information processing hierarchy of the human brain system. As noted earlier, in any complex system that is concerned with the expenditure of energy, mechanisms that are turned on first understandably gain significant power and leverage. Moreover, the Default system further embeds itself by associating the "objects" identified by the OIO system with memories of associated "objects". Because of the influence of the S/R system, many of these associations are linked to personal, and often emotionally charged memories, which elicit quick, defensive reactions. In psychological circles, this is often referred to as "triggering", and it happens to all of us. For example, a comment ("object"), however innocently made by a spouse might be associated with (i.e. "triggers") a memory of a similar comment ("object") made by a parent in a particular context that was emotionally difficult at the time. (A terrifying, exhilarating, disgusting, sad, joyous, etc. experience has been shown to elicit faster and stronger memory recall of such events than ordinary ones, and it seems likely that this set of dynamics also makes it easier for the Default system to associate current "objects" with ones that have been consciously experienced or otherwise unconsciously processed before.) This "triggering" process virtually thrusts us into a default, reactionary way of being, and it takes some effort to escape it, which is why many people refer to this set of events as "pushing my buttons" (if it involves someone else), or "running my tapes" (if one is doing it to him/herself).

On top of these two factors, the Default system is also where most of the effects of the brain system heuristics and biases discussed in Chapter Four come into play. For example, the Default system is highly prone to the Availability heuristic, which tends to exaggerate the importance of data and information that is immediately available rather than difficult to retrieve. In a system that is oriented toward self-preservation, information processing speed and energy conservation are always critical, and the Default system is therefore predisposed to consider the most immediately available *relevant* information.

For similar reasons, the Default system is also susceptible to the biases of "scarcity", loss aversion, and negativity. If energy conservation is paramount, building in systems dynamics that horde and seek to avoid unnecessary loss makes sense. And it also makes sense that such a system would be highly sensitized to information that warns of potential loss, or what the Default system would treat as "negative", while ascribing to it more weight than it would otherwise warrant. Unfortunately, what makes sense to a complex adaptive human brain system may not always serve the purposes of an even more complex adaptive brain/mind, which has to deal not only with issues of physical survival but social and psychological ones as well. Most of us know all too well the downside of living with a mind driven by scarcity mentality, aversion to loss, and negative perspectives on life.

Moreover, because the closed-loop dynamics of the Default system are so often self-oriented, they also run afoul of the human brain heuristics that confabulate food, money, and other desired "objects", like social status. A Default system that is largely preoccupied with preserving the integrity of the self will necessarily pursue strategies, behaviors, and thinking that seek to defend not just material possessions but intangible assets like social status, professional reputation, and interpersonal relationships. Default thinking usually contains some element of defensiveness.

Finally, three other closely related phenomena also have a great impact on the mechanics, dynamics, and outputs of the Default system. First, there is the issue of cognitive laziness. As we saw in Chapter Four, to conserve energy and process information as efficiently as possible, the human brain system lays down certain "expectations" of the stimuli and data it anticipates receiving, and in like fashion the entire Default system generates operating efficiency by looking for information that already confirms what it "understands" and "knows".

This Confirmation bias unfortunately also quite insidiously supports and reinforces yet another bias in the human brain/mind related to control and confidence—when the emergent mind senses itself in control, it gains confidence, and vice versa. The net effect of all these reinforcing dynamics manifests itself clearly in the thinking we encounter every day, whereby people who are operating out of their Default systems 1) just continue to look for information that confirms what they already know and believe, 2) find ways to gain power and control with those thought processes, and 3) continue to gain confidence that they are right, both in their thinking and their belief that such thinking should be allowed to control whatever issue is at stake. And to make matters more egregious still, such people tend to support all of this thinking with a particular set of moral heuristics, in which the ends always justify the means. Remember, all these dynamics and thinking emanate from the Default system and therefore tend to take on self-oriented, personal, emotional, and subjectively defensive influences. Sadly, we see this behavior and thinking every day in our politicians, who are positive that they are right about some issue, will not listen to any new information or point of view, and often sit on some moral high horse, vehemently defending a position in which the ends justify the means. (Only later, in some cases, to be thrown off those high horses by particularly lurid scandals and ironically hoisted by their own petards!)

Because the Default system is so highly dominated by the OIO and S/R systems, its information processing and distribution structure operates more like a "Scale Free" network, where a few nodes dominate and create highly centralized nodes, as discussed in Chapter Three. (The "nodes" of the Scale Free network in this case would actually be the major information processing networks within the OIO and S/R systems themselves.) While this Scale Free structure means the Default system can process and distribute critical pieces of information faster than would be true in a "Small World" network, it can also create nasty feedback loops, where thoughts just keep going around and around, swirling through the mind and often taking on negative energy.

Emergent phenomena of the Default system

Being emergent, the S/R system and the "self" that it gives rise to are entirely illusory—not in the sense that they do not exist or have great influence on the content of our minds, but illusory in the sense that we allow ourselves to think that this "self" represents who we are, whereas in truth it is only an emergent phenomenon of the S/R and Default systems. This represents perhaps the most interesting irony within the nature of humanity and the functioning of the human brain system—the S/R system and the "self" it generates are "strongly" emergent, so they can indeed "make choices" and direct a good measure of the mind's thoughts and chosen behaviors, but at the same time, they are entirely illusory. In other words, we choose how much power to give this illusory "self" and the tendencies that it gravitates toward, based on how much we use the Default system to process information and drive our thinking or behaviors. We cannot choose whether or not to allow our OIO to work—it is hardwired and designed to work under all circumstances, in order to improve our chances of survival—but we can choose how much energy we will give to the workings of the emergent S/R system and illusory "self". As will be discussed later in the section on the Integrated system, we can choose a different "self" than the one that emerges from the Default system alone.

Once we become aware of this set of dynamics and think about them, empowering the S/R system and allowing the illusory "self" to "run the show" and control our decision making creates its own "closed system". For example, it may be the larger Default system that "perceives" a piece of chocolate on the kitchen table, catalogues it as a "desirable" "object", associates it with pleasurable memories of eating chocolate in the past, and predicts that eating this chocolate would generate a "rewarding" feeling. But it is ultimately the S/R system and its emergent self that "make the decision" to eat it and then subsequently evaluate how "rewarding" an experience it was. In typical feedforward/feedback system fashion, the more this process occurs, the more it is reinforced in the neural networks, circuits, and systems involved in the process, and the "stronger" it becomes embedded. Strongly embedded systems veer toward becoming closed systems, which means that as long as the Default system is dominating, the illusory "self" will continue to simply assess the perceived "value" of the "reward" experienced by eating the chocolate, without questioning whether it is even a desired reward or could be replaced by some other type of food. A closed system at work.

Within this emergent self, we might include such other phenomena as ego and autobiographical self. The ego is the aspect of self that seems to generate its own emergent properties and goals or desires, making it easy for certain memes to embed themselves firmly in our minds. The autobiographical self seems to add the additional context of what we have been and still aspire to be, or do, which can also drive a good deal of the mind's emergent thinking. The emergent self of the Default system seems to carry with it a basic consciousness that concerns itself with preservation and conservation, which in turn often gives rise to limited, fixed mindsets, and a clear orientation toward self, first and foremost. These mindsets can obviously have a significant effect on the thinking that emerges within the brain/mind. On top of that, because the OIO "objectifies" everything, the Default system tends to gravitate toward very concrete, linear cause and effect thinking.

The Default system's thought processes

In addition to the ways that various brain system heuristics and bias affect the thinking that emerges when the Default system is in control, as explained earlier, Default thinking is also affected by specific mental thought processes that emerge from the particular dynamics of the Default system. For example, the OIO system generates a simple algorithm that says "if you find this object, associate it with this object, or not, depending on the similarity in the objects' characteristics". The S/R system places all those associations in the context of what has happened to the emergent "self" over time, and that type of "linear" thinking tends to reinforce self-referential, emotionally charged feelings, often creating a closed loop "tape" that repeats the same idea, thought, or feeling over and over again. I expect most people are quite familiar with this experience, whether it's the nagging notion that you forgot to close the garage door when you left in the morning, the persistent echo of why the boss just does not seem to like you, or the ubiquitous worry about whether you really have what it takes to do something that you deeply aspire to. Default thinking can be brutally automatic, concrete, mindlessly self-effacing, and viciously depressing, and because it is the default modality, it can completely devastate a person's thought processes. And even when it's not devastating, Default thinking can seep into all our mental processes and generate some insidious effects. Every day, we make a lot of poor associations and even worse judgments, completely unaware that we simply allowed our Default systems to make a series of extrapolations from past experiences.

Default thinking is based on the notion that there is a physical external reality, where cause and effect dynamics create linear relationships that can be used to predict future conditions or events. This is particularly true with interpersonal relationships, because they feed so easily into self-referential, emotional thinking. So we get easily trapped in the thinking that because our parents, spouses, friends, bosses, etc. treated us a certain way in the past, they will continue the exact same patterns in the future. (Sadly, thanks to family systems dynamics, they often do, but that is another story.) This is the aspect of Default thinking that so often prevents us from asking important questions of our doctors, family members, co-workers, and commercial vendors. As the great philosopher Heraclitus famously pointed out, we never step in the same river twice—things are always changing, so why don't we ask about what might have changed, instead of assuming that the way things were when we last checked in will be the way they are now? These are the perils of Default thinking.

Because it relies so heavily on the OIO system's "object" identification and cataloguing processes, Default thinking tends to compartmentalize things. Just like Split-Brain patients experience disjointed realities but invariably generate explanations designed to make sense of them, the Default system always seeks to reconcile many "objects" that it makes associations on, so it compartmentalizes them. For example, the "object" of "free speech" cannot always be reconciled in the Default system with the "object" catalogued as "loyalty", so the Default system compartmentalizes them, thereby avoiding having to associate and reconcile them in situations where the exercise of free speech would clearly be disloyal. In like fashion, the "object" of American culture that promotes individual material success cannot be associated, or reconciled, with any "object" of Christian belief that the rich must take care of the poor, so the Default thinking that goes on in many wealthy American Christian minds becomes highly compartmentalized, isolating potentially conflicting "objects" that emerge from within both of those belief systems.

Peter A. Schuller

Consistent with its concrete, objectified, compartmentalized characteristics, Default thinking also tends to traffic in "either/or" analyses, predictions, and programmed solutions. Obviously, either/or thinking creates serious limitations, especially in a world where quantum systems suggests that reality is often undefined and uncertain.

Additionally, studies involving the PCC suggest that the feedback loops that are generated within it are very firmly entrenched, and it seems possible that the network clusters that form within the Default system brain components would carry high "degree assortativity", meaning they are predisposed to making fast and firmly embedded associations between "objects". If this is true, insights from network science suggest that the PCC, and therefore the Default system generally, would be inclined to almost permanently fix in a person's mind all sorts of associations, warranted or not. While we know that we are hardwired to associate people of different races with specific characteristics and traits, this "assortative" quality of the Default system generates a much wider range of limiting, often pernicious mindsets and thinking. Western mindsets now seem particularly oriented toward placing labels on people and organizations and fixing various associations to those labels, which certainly can lure many people further into the trap of relying on Default system thinking.

Networked thinking, on the other hand, probably begins with an awareness and appreciation that Default thinking has obvious limitations, together with the realization that it stems from a certain mindset, which can always be changed. Choosing one's state of mind starts with the recognition that, being emergent and illusory, the self can be reined in. It does not have to dominate our goal making or our thinking. We can choose to alter our perceptions of the events around us, to make them less self-centered, and to widen the scope of our perspectives. We cannot stop the OIO or S/R systems from working—nor would we want to—but we can choose not to be ruled by them. Interestingly, one of the key exercises of those who practice "mindfulness" involves actually focusing on the outputs of the OIO system but simply maintaining attention on the actual outputs themselves, rather than allowing the S/R system and other parts of the Default system to generate countless self-oriented associations and other distracting thoughts.

Networked thinking allows the human brain system to open up all its "integrated" capacities and creativity. Over the last two decades, fMRI studies performed on expert meditators proves that it is possible to "tap down" the activities of the Default system in the back of the brain and shift the focus of mental activity toward the cognitive systems in the front, where the key components of the Integrated system are located.

Integrated system

The Integrated System offers an entirely different set of cognitive assets and orientations, as suggested by the characteristics listed in Figure 4 and the graphic resented below in Figure 6. Most of its key subsystems are located in the anterior part of the brain, including the most evolutionary recent addition to the human brain system, the neo-cortex, which makes possible functional capacities for logical reasoning, visualization, self-reflective consciousness, imagination, will, language, social and emotional judgment, critical decision making, and other mental tools that are unique to humans. Using these mental tools, the human mind is also able to take stock of a given situation; catalogue the various strategic options that might be available to address the demands of that situation; anticipate the consequences of each option; reassess the value of previously chosen strategies; and adopt another more appropriate course of action. In other words, by fully deploying our brain's Integrated system, we are able to make complex and sophisticated predictions, freely choose a course of action, and make continual adaptations to it.

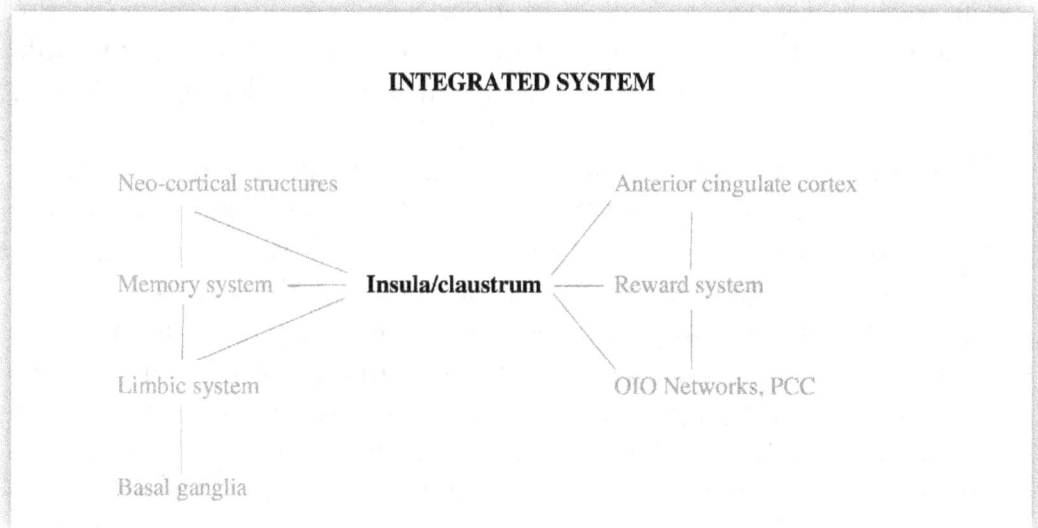

The contradistinction between the human brain's Default and Integrated systems is not quite the same as the differences that emerge between the brain's left and right hemispheres. As Figure 5 makes clear, the Default system is not separate and discrete from all other systems and capacities of the human brain system; it is not isolated in some way that would disconnect it from the Integrated system's capacity for reasoning, judgment, and the exercise of free will. It is more a question of when and how the tendencies embedded in the Default get reinforced over and over, leading to a form of "phase transition", whereby access to the full functionality of the Integrated system becomes increasingly less likely. Armed with a normal, healthy human brain system, one never gets completely stuck in either "left brain" or "right brain" thinking, but there is no doubt that one can get mired in Default system thinking, unable to access all the sophisticated capacities of the Integrated system and the open-minded thinking it engenders.

Moreover, whereas the Default system tends to be highly influenced by the OIO and S/R systems, which often cause it to become very self-oriented and recursive, the Integrated system is geared toward coordinating all the necessary functional components of the Default system with the higher level, evolutionarily more recent functionalities embedded in the neo-cortex. Accordingly, the Integrated system operates in a more balanced, functionally broad set of dynamics than does the Default system. It is more geared toward collaboration and cooperation than the Default system is. As represented in Figure 6, note also how the Integrated system introduces a whole new set of *networked* capabilities, which lays the foundation for a much more open, future-oriented, strategic way of thinking than could possibly occur by relying on the dynamics of the Default system.

From the standpoint of systems analysis, the Integrated system does a lot more than coherently tie together the functional exigencies of the Default system, the motivational implications of the "reward system" (discussed below), and the higher order capacities of the neo-cortex. The Integrated system operates as a both complex adaptive system and a sophisticated information sharing network. It integrates information sets and creates critically important patterns of networked information, in order to generate complex outputs, much in the same way that the dedicated visual processing centers in different brain regions (V1 through V6) operate in parallel and stitch together the key aspects of sensory stimuli in order to construct our mental images of the "outside world". Quite possibly, it is this type of cross-brain functional integration that gives rise to our most sophisticated "emergent" capabilities, such as self-reflective consciousness, existential free will, sense of a "higher self", and the like.

We do know, for example, that electromagnetic wave coherence at 40 Hz is observed across the entire brain system, which may evidence certain aspects of observed human consciousness.

Perhaps most importantly, the Integrated system gives rise to all the major aspects of mind that make humans so unique. I do not mean just the mental tools mentioned above, which represent some of the interdependent, networked components that provide such wide ranging, emergent functionality to the human mind. I mean aspects of mind that make it capable of generating its own desires, rewards, and plans, *independent* of what might be going on within the moment to moment operational dynamics of the underlying brain system. For example, as noted below, the human brain system operates a "reward system" that is geared primarily to processing information that is relevant to the predictions and strategies the brain system is relying on to survive and adapt. But at the same time that the brain is engaged in such activities, the human mind can redirect the brain's activities to call up "objects" identified and catalogued in its memory systems and manipulate them to create incentives or lay out desired "rewards" for future reference. The mind can "say" to itself, freely and independently, "If I make myself go work out for 30 minutes, I can reward myself with an ice cream". There may indeed be biochemical and neuronal network wiring predilections that might factor into what actually happens—for example, low blood sugar, which might make concentration difficult or press the immediate desire to eat something rather than work, but the mind is still ultimately in control of whether or not the 30 minutes of work is performed right then and there, based on the anticipated reward.

Just to make sure I am clear on this point, I am not going down the particular rabbit hole that is portrayed in the movie *The Matrix* or suggesting that the human mind can ever operate completely untethered from the brain system that gives rise to it. Indeed, because of a person's particular genome and body chemistry, eating ice cream might turn into a less than enjoyable experience, perhaps from a reaction based on lactose intolerance, in which case the mind would eventually not even contemplate it as a desired reward. But this is more a case of the human brain/body system altering certain premises in the mind *after the fact*, rather than injecting some set of neuronal or biochemical mechanics that might obviate the mind's decision making in the first place. With this in mind (pun intended), let's take a further look into how the emergent phenomena generated by the Integrated system might affect the nature and applications of networked thinking.

If the Default system generates an "illusory self" and a self-oriented mindset, then the Integrated system seeks to bring forth a self-aware, "authentic self" and an other-oriented mindset. Based on recent studies, it appears that neural networks and circuits within the Integrated system, like those contained in the claustrum and the insula, provide the emergent mind and "authentic self" with particular capacities for self-awareness and consciousness, empathy, self-regulation, and sophisticated models for assessing risk and reward. A brain that is operating primarily within the Default system would have difficulty sustaining such emergent capacities of mind.

Moreover, the Integrated system generates and sustains what Carol Dweck calls a "growth mindset", which means it produces emergent properties like positive attitudes, ambition, and self-reflective consciousness. Unlike the self-preservation oriented consciousness generated by the Default system, self-reflective consciousness directs the mind toward an "internal reality" that can be freely changed. This clearly has a major impact on one's perceptions of, and perspectives on his or her reality. While the Default system relies heavily on the objectified outputs of the OIO system to generate a perception of "external reality" that must be assessed and adapted to, the Integrated system gives rise to a highly dynamic, internally generated perspective, which can be adjusted in an instant. And as we have already seen, once the mind adjusts its perception of reality, it can precipitate (top down) shifts in the underlying brain system. The Integrated system promotes the emergence of critical human phenomena like imagination, vision, and courage, which in turn generate their own particular causal influences on the ever-repeating cycle of our key cognitive processes: *perception—attention—information processing—memory—consciousness—perception.*

The growth mindset and self-reflective consciousness that emerge by engaging the Integrated system allow for the development of what are now being called "emotional" and "social" intelligence. A mind that is in touch with its authentic self and able to reflect clearly on its internal reality has the wherewithal to take full account of and manage the entire range of emotional states and events. Similarly, such a mind is free to see and listen to others without distraction, practice the empathy that all humans are hardwired for, and even exercise true compassion. And as this occurs, the entire process reinforces the orientation of the emergent mind toward the existence, concerns, and thoughts of others. So, just as the Default system sends the mind and its thoughts into the rabbit hole that is the preservation of the self, the Integrated system opens the mind and its thinking to a more "other oriented" possibility, all of which makes a great difference when it comes to other facets of human thinking, such as predictive and strategic.

The Integrated system's thought processes

A growth mindset and open mind generates a predilection toward learning and adaptive thinking. With self-reflective consciousness comes the ability to analyze facts and distinguish them readily from opinion, which necessarily reflects the limitations of someone's experiences, perspectives, and knowledge. Open-mindedness not only allows for "holistic thinking" but gives rise to an appreciation of nuance; the capacity for mindfulness; an interest in securing diverse sources of information; the desire to learn, especially from earlier miscalculations (as opposed to "mistakes"); the ability to persevere in pursuit of a vision; the freedom to allow "Bayesian updating" to take place and drive strategic thinking; and many other manifestations of "free will" that simply cannot find form within the dynamics of the Default system. As one might expect, all of these factors influence the thought processes that emerge from within the Integrated system.

Moreover, the very holistic nature of the Integrated system may also give rise to extended capacities of thought. For example, fully accessing the Integrated system may help us enhance our *intuitive* thought processes. A recent study has linked intuition with the caudate nucleus, which is part of the basal ganglia, an integral component of the limbic system that is thought to be responsible for learning and executing habitual behavior. The basal ganglia receives considerable input from the cortical regions of the brain and projects back into those areas in well-designed feedback loops, suggesting that it contributes highly to conscious perception and analysis of any given situation. The caudate nucleus is therefore thought to play a central role in the capacity of "experts" to come up with insightful answers without conscious thought. ("Experts" in this case might well equate to the meaning Malcolm Gladwell intends when he refers, in *Outlier*, to people who have gained over 10,000 hours of training in a given skill or domain of expertise.) Allowing our brain systems to operate in their fully integrated modes clearly would increase the likelihood that intuitive type thoughts generated through the functionality of the caudate nucleus would not only be generated within the basal ganglia but find free and consistent expression.

Perhaps another way to look at the thinking that emerges from full deployment of the Integrated system and the "open" mind that emerges from it is through an "Information centric" model, as described in the following points:

- An open, holistic mind encourages the free flow of Random Information, diversity of Ordered Information, and accumulation of "knowledge" (in the form of experience and acquired knowledge bases).
- That optimizes the potential for the brain system's "genetic algorithms" to generate valuable new "ideas".
- These processes encourage thinking that are geared toward open-ended possibility and avoids the Default system's simple formula of extrapolation from the past, where "whatever happened before will happen the same way again."
- This more "open" kind of thinking promotes curiosity, clarity of observation, and knowledge based perception, which is essential for making good decisions.
- After all, one cannot choose something that one does not know exists. Creative, even "out of the box", thinking requires knowledge of how things work and what might be possible.
- Open and creative thinking encourages proactive choosing and decision making, which in turn avoids the limitations created by the "path of least resistance" that is so often found in the Default system.
- Ultimately, the form of proactive, existential choice that emerges by fully deploying the Integrated system gives rise to virtual loops of positive reinforcement that: 1) perpetuate the dynamics of an "open mind", 2) allow for the emergence of thinking and decision making that can exist independent of what is going on in the underlying brain system, and 3) enhance the efficiency of the Integrated system's Small World information processing networks and their capacity for distributing both Random and Ordered Information.

Key Component systems

Both the Default and Integrated systems contain major component systems that they use to achieve their respective goals, though the effects and outputs produced by such component systems may vary greatly, depending on whether the Default or Integrated system is dominating and what mindset, or consciousness, is predominating at any given moment. Because networked thinking is tied closely to the dynamics of the human brain system's reward and memory systems, I will focus on those two component systems.

Reward system

Being a multi-functional, predictive system that uses many different kinds of feedforward and feedback systems to set and pursue goals, learn, and adapt, the human brain system relies heavily on a diverse and versatile form of "reward" system. Neuroscientists are still trying to work out the full measure of this system, but it seems clear that it both 1) enables the brain to consistently identify new, relevant information and 2) generates within the mind a range of subjectively "rewarding" experiences, which presumably are tied directly to the dynamics of motivation. For example, certain taste sensations produce "rewarding" feelings in some people, some of the time, but not in others; some people are motivated to exercise by the "rewarding" feelings of endorphin release that comes from it, while others do not experience the same rewarding feeling and therefore remain less motivated to pursue exercise. To borrow from Damasio's three tier construct for human consciousness discussed in the last chapter, it may well be that there are distinctly different reward systems that correspond to levels and types of consciousness, but we still have a long way to go in sorting that out.

Regardless of whether the human brain's reward system produces feel good sensations that our minds interpret as subjectively "rewarding", it always makes our brain systems pay attention to novelty. Even one month old infants automatically focus on things that are new and different. Presumably, this one function ensures that our brain systems are always alert to and ready to process data and information that are relevant to the countless predictions those brain systems are making every moment. Interestingly, this is exactly what Information Theory itself would predict. As noted in Chapter Two, the amount of Information in any given message is proportional to the improbability of the message content, and apparently our human brain systems are constantly scanning for new information precisely because it contains the most Information, within the context of Information Theory.

The primary driver of this reward system seems to involve the release of dopamine molecules. Dopamine is a monoamine neurotransmitter that is synthesized from the amino acid tyrosine by dopaminergic cells located primarily in the midbrain. From these nuclei, neuronal projections extend into the dorsal striatum and the limbic cortex, especially the nucleus accumbens and the amygdala, the latter two of which are considered the primary substrates for reward processing. Dopamine molecules operate as strategic neurotransmitters in the formation and reinforcement of neural pathways that generate "learning" and updating of the brain system's predictive models. But this "learning" does not always occur in the form of direct cause and effect, as we have come to think of it, for example, in the famous case of Pavlov's dog. Behaviorally, the dog, being enticed by the treat, learned to associate the sound of the bell with the release of the treat, in direct cause and effect. Inside its brain, on the other hand, when the bell was first rung and the treat followed, there was a release of dopamine molecules that prompted the brain to not only pay particular attention to this new information but also begin to discard any other previously relevant information. In other words, just like our own, the dog's reward system consistently prompted it to pinpoint information that was relevant by discarding that was not (e.g. earlier conditions under which he received food outside of normal feeding cycles). Call it addition by subtraction, a concept that factors into network thinking as well.

There are several important implications to this set of dynamics. First, we must be careful about how we think about all the associations our brain systems make, especially in terms of what our minds assess as simple cause and effect. As pointed out in Chapter Four, our brain systems are usually pressed for time and energy, so they like to take shortcuts, and one of the most common (and potentially misguided) ones is assuming simple cause and effect associations, even when they do not exist. Someone speaks harshly to us, and we assume it's because of something we did rather than what might be going on in that other person's life that makes it difficult and stressful. If we had an unlimited amount of time in life and our brains had energy to spare, our brains might be more inclined to seek out ALL the available relevant information, which would allow our minds to contemplate an entire spectrum of causal explanations for the events of our lives, but the truth that they simply cannot. And so we must discipline our minds to investigate thoroughly the many possible reasons for what happens in life, not just the apparent cases of simple cause and effect.

Second, a dopamine based reward system that signals different strategic systems in the brain when new and relevant information is received can be leveraged to provide two important sources of "drive": 1) attention and learning, and 2) motivation through incentivizing.

Attention and learning is vital to the human brain system and its fundamental predictive mechanisms. It is thought that dopamine is required for formation of associations with reward-related stimuli and reward predictions, as a fundamental mechanism through which most organisms optimize the pursuit of natural rewards that are essential for survival, such as food and water. Moreover, it has been proposed that dopamine activity drives attention and learning by encoding reward expectation, or more specifically errors in reward expectation, as evidenced by findings that both dopaminergic cells and downstream striatal neurons will modulate their firing in response to predictors of reward, prior to receipt of the reward itself. Recent research by a team led by Roberto Malinow of the University of California, San Diego, suggests that the relevant information from this event is further processed in the lateral habenula as some form of "disappointment" that prompts adjustments to the brain system's predictive models and the strategies devised by the mind to become "smarter" about the next set of trials.

As it relates to the second drive, motivation through incentivizing, current theory suggests that the principal role of dopamine is to attribute incentive salience to rewards and reward-related stimuli. In other words, dopamine release signals the brain that some rewards may be more relevant than others, depending on the current state of the brain system itself, or the particular conditions of the environment at the time. It may well be that such incentive salience is modulated in the brain through neuroadaptations that effectively help embed this form of reward based learning, which appears to take place in the lateral striatum.

This raises two interesting questions in terms of networked thinking and human decision making in general. First, we ought to ask ourselves how much this very incentive oriented reward system translates into qualities and tendencies of the emergent mind. Are not our minds somewhat relativistic? Surely, we do not experience the rewards we think we seek the same way all the time. After the fifth bite of chocolate cake, our minds are not as anxious to take the next bite as they were the first one. On the third consecutive annual trip to Florida, our minds do not experience the same level of excited anticipation as they did originally. Even after the second or third consecutive sporting tournament win, our minds begin to lose the sensation of reward. Perhaps in the mind, this effect represents the other side of the same coin involving expectations generated by our brain systems—I imagine that most of us have had more than a few experiences where the expectations and anticipation of what we hoped would be our reward for engaging in a particular project proved to be far more gratifying than the putative reward itself.

Second, we ought to exercise that wonderful capacity for self-reflective consciousness that is so unique to the human species and ask ourselves whether we even know what "rewards" we think we are pursuing. As we have seen, the human brain has its own set of reward systems dynamics, but by the very nature of its emergent characteristics, the human mind can intervene and make its own choices. It is the nature of our free will that we make the effort to study what our brains are doing, understand the consequence of these mechanics, ask ourselves reflectively whether that suits the ambitions and desires we have generated, then choose a different path, a different set of "rewards".

For example, maybe just like our brain systems, our minds do find "learning" rewarding, both for its adaptive value and for the intrinsic sense of satisfaction it seems to generate. But what kind of "learning"? Learning the "hard way"? Learning by ourselves, or in community? Or maybe learning from mindful, thoughtful consideration of what we truly value in life, what we really seek to accomplish with the gifts and talents we have acquired. I expect that most people like to learn, in one fashion or another, but it never hurts to understand why, or how, that might be true in any particular case. Given how hard won most of our significant rewards in life are, we ought to at least exercise enough free will to consciously pursue rewards that actually serve our goals and ambitions.

Memory systems

Memory seems to be one of the truly indispensable functions in the entire complex adaptive dynamics of the human brain system. Without a clear memory of what has gone on before, it would be virtually impossible to make the predictions our human brain system must generate every second to survive. Moreover, memory of past experiences, learned procedures, and other key facts such as what parents and friends look like, are essential to the emergence of many critical human phenomena, such as agency, sense of autobiographical self, and even consciousness.

The system of human memory is generally broken down into three major categories: Sensory, Short Term (known as Working Memory), and Long Term, which itself carries several distinctions: Explicit (conscious) vs. Implicit (unconscious); Declarative (which in turn can be either Semantic or Episodic), vs. Procedural.

Sensory Memory allows the nervous system and the brain system to retain the information embedded in sensory stimuli long enough to be transferred to Working Memory. Working Memory represents the "mental blackboard" that allows our minds to hold onto specific data and information long enough to manipulate it for some specific calculus, then store the results in long-term memory. Declarative memory, what most people think of when they consider the dynamics of human memory, involves our very sophisticated capacity for storing and recalling the events of our lives and the countless facts and circumstances that give rise to the "context" (or semantic meaning) for our lives. Procedural memory allows us to learn and remember how to do certain things, such as ride a bike; often those memories are relegated to the subcortical regions of the brain that process rote behaviors. Semantic memory involves the recording and recall of facts, ideas, concepts, and the like, while episodic memory is what lets us record and recall past events and experiences.

While the hippocampus plays a major role in the encoding, consolidation, storage, and recall of long-term memories, most of these processes are widely distributed throughout the human brain system's various networks and circuits. These processes are not fully integrated, however, and the networks used for memory encoding and storage of a given memory are different from those used to recall the same memory. Accordingly, the storing of a memory represents a distinctly different neural event from the recalling of that memory, which may or may not accurately reflect the facts and circumstances that were actually stored into memory originally. Moreover, every memory recall is a new process, which can generate a different experience than the one that emerged during the previous recall of the same memory. Clearly, human memory recall is an imperfect process, quite unlike the retrieval of data from a computer. By contrast, the human brain's memory systems *are* highly integrated with its emotional processing systems, thereby generating important "evaluative" labels that seem to endure with great fidelity for long periods of time. The clearest memory recalls are often the ones most tinged with emotion.

From the vantage point of networked thinking, the human brain's memory system several important issues. Being itself a highly networked system, it calls into question exactly what happens when we engage in declarative memory recall and how that affects not only our thinking but how we share our "knowledge" with others. Is that "knowledge" sound or based on the recall of facts and circumstances that are badly distorted during recall? We know that declarative memory is highly distributed throughout the brain, but we certainly don not have a good map of that network, so we really cannot say how much the key placement of a "weak tie" here or a "strong tie" there affects how we might recall a given piece of our "knowledge".

Memory is also foundational to our consciousness, which affects our perceptions, perspectives, and ultimately what we might choose to store in memory, or recall later. There are so many moving parts to the process of human thinking, starting with countless aspects of consciousness and ending with the vagaries of mood, brain bio-chemistry, and the like. Accordingly, we ought always to remain mindful of how complex the human memory system is, how much it factors into the even more complex process of thinking, and how such thinking in turn affects what remembered "knowledge" we share with others.

PART III—NETWORKED THINKING

8

NETWORKED THINKING IN THE HUMAN BRAIN SYSTEM

The primary purpose of this book is to uncover the characteristics, processes, and practices of networked thinking, so that we might apply it to become better thinkers, decision makers, and communicators, while adding to the depth and breadth of human intelligence. As hopefully should be clear by now, the human mind, and the thought processes that emerge within it, are amazing phenomena that can both generate original "ideas" and act as agents in the open-ended process by which Information self-organizes in culture (memes). Networked thinking aims to take full advantage of how networks process information, especially within the human brain system, while avoiding the pitfalls of both the human brain's Default system and the distracting messages embedded in memes, as they emerge and spread within human culture.

Networked thinking is not just about what happens in the individual human brain system and mind. It also involves the dynamics of how many different minds communicate together, in networks. By deploying the insights of network science and complexity science, as applied to organizations, we can use networked thinking to generate a novel approach to organizational development, which is the subject of the next chapter.

Before we talk about the nature and characteristics of networked thinking and how it can change our decision making, it will be useful to engage in a quick summary of the key points we have established so far, particularly as they relate to networked thinking.

- *The human brain is a self-organizing (and therefore complex adaptive) system that is highly impacted by the dynamics of Information Theory and its implications in connection with the 1) performance of entropy reducing Work, 2) processing of both Random and Ordered Information, and 3) dynamics of how Information self-organizes in human culture (memes).*

- *As a complex adaptive system, the human brain generates some very unique "strong" emergent phenomena, including the mind, consciousness, self, will, ego, and thought, which necessarily create new levels of organization within that system, extending its adaptive capabilities and ability to "learn".*
- *As a complex adaptive system, the human brain relies on a tremendous number of both simple and sophisticated feedforward and feedback systems, providing it with an unparalleled ability to synthesize and organize Information, in order to further enhance its capacities for learning and adaptation.*
- *As a complex adaptive system that has many different functions and therefore consumes considerable energy, the human brain system relies on a hierarchical network of information processing and distribution networks, using four distinct structures: Random, Ordered, Small World, and Scale Free; Small World (primarily neural) networks are the most efficient and stable of these structures, so they represent the predominant network structure, especially in the brain's Integrated system. (The human brain's Default and Integrated systems create two different sets of operational dynamics, which affect the mechanics and outputs of their respective information processing networks.)*
- *These Small World networks use patterns of information stored within the human brain system, as well as random, novel sets of information from its external environment, and apply "genetic algorithms" to produce new "ideas" and potential solutions to pressing challenges from the environment.*
- *Because of how the human brain system's emergent phenomena self-organize hierarchically, when such "ideas" are manipulated in different human thinking processes, they have a "strong" downward effect on the state and content of the mind, which in turn affects the operational (and sometimes even the structural) dynamics of the underlying human brain system.*
- *Networked thinking takes all of these factors into account and focuses on the way information self-organizes and is processed within different systems in the human brain, as well as how the information flowing through its Small World networks can be manipulated to generate more effective thinking and more strategic decision making.*

So, networked thinking is ultimately focused on the flow of information, whether Random or Ordered, within the human brain system and how it can be managed to generate new "ideas". In some cases, this means avoiding the restrictive dynamics of the brain's Default system or readjusting the focus of its Reward system, so as to improve the self-organizing influx of both Random and Ordered Information. In other cases, it means generating critical syntheses from feedback systems and recirculating the outputs from such syntheses throughout the brain system's key information processing mechanisms. Networked thinking involves both addition by subtraction and addition from adaptive innovation.

Networked thinking takes into account the network effect of the following phenomena: 1) the organizing "Work" that complex adaptive systems—and in particular our brain systems and social systems—perform to reduce the effects of entropy that naturally emerge within such systems; 2) how Information self-organizes in such complex adaptive systems; 3) how the human brain system generates key emergent phenomena of mind, consciousness, etc. to optimize our human capacity to adapt; 4) how feedforward and feedback systems in the human brain synthesize Information to generate "learning"; and 5) how the human brain system uses network dynamics and genetic algorithms to generate critical adaptive "ideas".

If we map these phenomena as nodes in a network, connected to each other by various weak and strong ties, we can track the network effect of how they affect human thinking. For example, strong ties connect our complex adaptive human brain system to the dynamics of meme generation and spreading, indicating that memes have a significant (and often unconscious) impact on our thinking. On the other hand, the adaptive learning that takes place in another person's brain/mind would only be connected to our own brain/mind through a weak tie, suggesting that it might have some effect on what we think and do, but it would not be lasting and consistent. (One of the intriguing issues of how we develop as humans stems from this very phenomenon—how it is that our brain/minds learn so effectively from their own predictive errors but so little from observing the "mistakes" of others.)

Moreover, we have seen how Information Theory dynamics dictate the way Information is processed and messages are encoded for transmittal, so it should come as no surprise that some individual brain/minds synthesize information better than others. Information synthesis in turn affects the adaptive and predictive strategies of the individual brain/mind, as well as determines how Random Information sets are manipulated by genetic algorithms and turned into "ideas". We might say that synthesized information in the individual brain/mind is connected, by weak ties, to nodes in the individual brain/mind that represent various forms of strategic, creative, and innovative thinking.

Each individual brain/mind gives rise to its own unique organizational structure, within the hierarchy of brain-mind-thinking, and accordingly generates a particular approach to thinking. Some brain systems are dominated by their Default systems, which produce a very narrow, concrete emergent mind, and in turn a limited range of thinking tools. That in turn affects the type of information synthesis that takes place in such brain/minds; it influences the types of memes that are implicitly and unconsciously copied within such brain/minds, then spread to other similar brain/minds; and it surely impacts the feedforward and feedback systems of such brain/minds, further reinforcing the organizational dynamics by which a Default system dominated brain gives rise to an unimaginative, concrete mind and linear, uncreative thinking.

To see exactly how this set of network effects drive the mechanics of network thinking, we need to take a closer look at what happens at the systems dynamics of the human brain/mind and what happens at each of the three organizational levels of the human brain-mind-thinking system.

Networked thinking and the limitations generated by the Default and Reward Systems

Default system driven thinking tends to generate fixed mindsets and concrete, linear, self-oriented thinking, which in turn generates the "downward" effect of reinforcing the brain system's innate tendency to look for information that confirms what it already "knows" and "expects". Such thinking literally forecloses the possibility of allowing in conflicting or random information that is vital innovative thought. From a network science perspective, the Default system tends to operate with a more Scale Free structure of information processing networks than does the Integrated system, which potentially limits a person's thinking to a limited number of *existing* ideas and thoughts. For example, someone's view on ethics might be guided by the Kantian notion of categorical imperatives, with all other related moral and ethical norms being connected to that one absolutist principle in a Scale Free network structure of related ethical concepts. If that person allows his brain's Default system to control his thinking related to an ethical issue, the concepts relevant to that issue will necessarily connect in his brain/mind to the overriding principle of categorical imperatives, which likely will foreclose consideration of concepts tied to other principles, such as those connected to situational ethics. Moreover, such Default system thinking will begin to affect other component systems, such as memory, which will tend to store only the facts and circumstances that support any particular ethical concept that derives from a categorical imperative.

Much the same occurs within the work processes of organizations. Hierarchically driven, entrenched management practices create the effect of a Scale Free information processing network, which taps into Default system thinking within the organization. Stakeholders learn to operate in an environment of established "truths", values, and principles, primary of which is to protect one's own stake within the organization. Personal knowledge is jealously guarded, and few undertake to synthesize and redistribute the many possible information sets that might lead to the emergence of new "ideas". In contradistinction, because the Integrated system tends to rely on Small World information processing and distribution structures, it preserves the possibility of either cracking open an entrenched belief system or obviating it altogether. Small World networks provide a more stable, diverse, and random base of information flow.

Networked thinking requires a highly intentional approach to the dynamics of reward in the human brain system and emergent mind, because of how reward-centric our thinking generally is. The human brain's reward system is geared to focusing its attention on new and relevant information, especially if it is at odds with an anticipated reward. Unmet expectations lead to dampened release of dopamine and engenders a sense of "disappointment" in the mind, none of which is conducive to creative and innovative thinking. Networked thinking therefore needs to tread a fine line between, on the one hand, a fundamental openness to new and relevant information, which the brain naturally scans for, and calculated pragmatism on the other. Nothing distracts human thinking more than experiencing the "disappointment" of anticipating one set of information and getting a completely different one instead. Networked thinking encourages the consistent monitoring of information types and sources, to make sure the brain/mind is exposed to a good balance of both novel and expected information.

Moreover, the human brain/mind is constantly being bombarded by memes, some of which are entirely geared toward defining what society deems to be desired rewards, whether small and temporary, such as the refreshing beer at the end of a long day, or more long term and image-oriented, such as the "Ultimate Driving Machine". Networked thinking requires that we remain mindful of how these memes influence both our brain systems and minds, driving them toward goals and objectives that we may either be not consciously aware of nor particularly satisfied with, once they have been achieved.

This is a particularly critical point because of how prone our brain systems and minds are to engage in habitual thinking and behavior. Remember, both our brains and minds have an incredible amount of work to do every second, and engaging in some measure of habit is literally the only way our brain systems can manage their workloads. Can you imagine having to think about everything you do while you are driving your car, as you navigate your way to work, or even just putting one foot in front of the other as you negotiate your office parking lot? Habits are by their nature deeply engrained processes—the brain system receives a cue, engages in a behavior, and receives the expected reward. That's it. If the reward does not eventuate, no habit is laid down in the first place, but once a pattern emerges that generates a conditioned response and a perceived reward, the habit becomes firmly embedded. Habits are essential, but habituated thinking can be very limiting.

Networked Thinking and the effect of strong emergence

Nothing better exemplifies the wondrous power of the human brain system or plays a more integral role in the emergence of networked thinking than the strongly emergent nature of the human mind. The human mind is uniquely self-aware, provides a consciousness of who we are, have been, and might be. It generates a mental space to make calculations, predictions, and contingent, adaptive strategies. It allows us to visualize what has not yet occurred, test a strategy, and make adjustments, well before a situation even presents itself. The list goes on and on, but perhaps most importantly, the emergent human mind provides us with a mechanism for "thinking" and making a wide range of choices, even including the choice to change one's thinking. Not just predictive and strategic thinking, but inductive, deductive, critical thinking; thinking that involves manipulating concepts and ideas; thinking that allows us to invent things and contemplate worlds that do not resemble our own.

Why is this so important? Because the demand for adaptation in modern human life is accelerating. So our thinking needs to become more agile, creative, and innovative. Using our strongly emergent minds to make good, adaptive choices requires high levels of intentionality and discipline. Remember that according to the dynamics of complex adaptive systems, even though "higher" level emergent phenomena have a strong, top down effect on the states of "lower" level emergent phenomena, they are also less predictable in nature. The less predictable mental phenomena are, the more important discipline becomes. For example, memes come and go quickly in our social and cultural environment, and it is virtually impossible to predict which ones will emerge within that environment or which ones will get stuck in our minds, so it requires extreme vigilance to choose the ones we will allow to guide our thoughts. I doubt that there is anyone who could have told you ten years ago how firmly embedded the Twitter meme would become in America, and there is certainly no one who could tell you today which Tweeted meme is going to "trend" most powerfully tomorrow. Being strongly emergent phenomena, our thoughts, and the concepts embedded in memes, are virtually impossible to predict but powerful in effect.

Networked Thinking and the effect of Small World network dynamics

The primary information processing structure in the Integrated system of the human brain system is a hierarchical nested set of Small World (primarily neural) networks. Because of their capacity to distribute information and knowledge cost efficiently while remaining resilient to internal node failure, the strong ties of Small World clusters exchange information quickly, making them particularly good at synthesizing key pieces of information and "feeding them forward" into the rest of the network, using weak ties to connect with the non-clustered nodes. Moreover, these clusters of nodes are effective at consolidating learning and knowledge bases, which are so essential to directing the attention of the mind and its underlying brain system—after all, we cannot think things that our minds do not believe exist. Small World networks give rise to diverse, robust knowledge bases that are easily shared, which is one of the keys to promoting networked thinking, either within the individual brain/mind, or in Knowledge Networks.

Small World (neural) networks promote the type of free-flowing, open, curious, and observant mind that facilitates the exercise of diversified, non-linear, and holistic thinking, all of which are foundational to networked thinking. Presumably, thanks to the cause and effect of networked thinking, its practice will also eventually promote increased reliance on the Integrated system and its Small World information processing networks, which in turn will improve the brain system's capacity for absorbing and synthesizing new information, be it Random or Ordered.

Networked Thinking and genetic algorithms

The mechanism behind the human brain system's capacity to build genetic algorithms and build new "ideas" lies in the application of strategically placed feedforward and feedback systems. This is particularly true when the human brain system manipulates different information patterns to represent derivative "objects", much in the same way gene mutations and meme variations generate the potential for new "ideas", which must then be tested for adaptive utility. The human brain/mind uses intricate feedforward systems to do its "testing", either by mentally projecting it into a designed application and calculating the possible consequences (as, for example, with a thought experiment) or by initiating a specific behavioral command, then deploying dedicated feedback systems to test the actual "fitness" of such behaviors in the appropriate environmental conditions.

The precise neural workings of how such genetic algorithms might produce "derivative objects" and test the fitness of the new "ideas" that emerge from manipulating them those "objects" remain unclear, though we might guess at them, using concepts like Jeff Hawkins' SDR model discussed in Chapter Four. The crux of this model is that three dimensional neural networks allow for virtually endless permutations and combinations of synaptic connections and neural conformations, each representing a bit, or bit combination, of Information. Essentially, as such neural conformations change, in the slightest rearrangements of time and space, countless "patterns" of Information are created, some of which are manipulated according to the mysterious factoring of the unconscious mind, then eventually made accessible to the conscious mind (what some might call "Eureka moments"). Thus, it seems possible that just as genetic mutation and "noise" are converted into new "ideas" that are tested for fitness within Nature's competitive landscape, new patterns of Information encoded in SDRs might generate new "objects" that could be manipulated in the human brain/mind to produce new thoughts, concepts, and other forms of "ideas".

Networked thinking characteristics

Human thinking is a powerful but erratic and unpredictable undertaking. The aim of networked thinking is not only to generate important new "ideas" and expand our collective human intelligence, but also to evolve a less erratic approach to thinking and decision making.

Human thinking has undergone some significant changes throughout the course of our evolution, and there is no reason why we should not experience several more. When the brain/minds of our ancestors generated the "idea" of written communication and "invented" the alphabet, it engendered a fundamental change in the dynamics of how we collect and share information, build knowledge, and develop intelligence. And with that change, we made it possible for our thinking to become both more logical and more imaginative. All of a sudden, thoughts and concepts could be analyzed, extended, and varied far more effectively and consistently than was ever possible with verbal communication alone. With the skills of written communication, humans could also read about, catalogue, compare, contrast, and associate different ways of thinking, giving rise to a whole new capability—the power to reason. Reading and rereading another person's thoughts is a totally different mental exercise than trying to understand what she was thinking while simultaneously struggling to remember exactly what she had said.

With written communication, the human brain could reorganize itself to support new analytical processes, not only enhancing its capacity for logical thought but adding capabilities of non-linear, critical, and imaginary thinking. Interestingly, it is now well-accepted that our brain systems did begin to rearrange themselves structurally with the advent of written language, becoming both more globally networked and more tightly connected within the neo-cortex, the seat of uniquely human intelligence. (It is of course, no coincidence that this "invention" of written language itself contains network phenomena—letters of the alphabet, at least in Western languages, tend to self-organize into an identifiable network structure to create words, and words self-organize into similar network structures to generate sentences. Accordingly, I have put "invention" in quotes to suggest that we might simply be agents of a self-organizing process from which the "idea" of written language eventually had to emerge.)

Written communication allowed us to gain a deeper understanding of who we are and what others think about, and it also significantly advanced our Theory of Mind. (This is the understanding that other people have their own perspectives, minds, and thoughts, which are necessarily different than our own, usually acquired by humans around age four.) We acquired more opportunities to share perspectives and broaden our own perceptions of reality. Changes that emerged within the human brain system following the invention of written communication doubtless even improved the human brain's capacity for "Bayesian updating", which means that it can use streams of new information to continually enhance its predictions of what might happen next. *Written* facts and figures are easier to record and manipulate in Working Memory, which would make them more accessible to the brain system's natural processes for Bayesian updating.

It may well be that the emergence of the new "idea" that is the Internet/Web has started to usher in another significant shift in human thinking and intelligence. And perhaps just as written language provided us with new mental tools and types of thinking processes, so the Internet/Web will give rise to a new collective "mental workspace" (similar in function to Working Memory in the individual brain system) that will help us enhance our practice of networked thinking, with all its attendant benefits. Perhaps the Internet/Web will enable us to increase our capacity for the kind of first-rate thinking that Keith Stanovich describes in his book, *What Intelligence Tests Miss:*

> *"The tendency to collect information before making up one's mind, the tendency to seek various points of view before coming to a conclusion, the disposition to think extensively about a problem before responding, the tendency to calibrate the degree of strength of one's opinions to the degree of evidence available, the tendency to think about future consequences before taking action, the tendency to explicitly weigh pluses and minuses of a situation before making a decisions, and the tendency to seek nuance and avoid absolutism."*

Without doubt, most people do not *consistently* display the kind of intelligence described by Stanovich, but we are definitely going down the right path, and we need to use networked thinking to keep moving us along it. Toward that end, we need to fully understand the characteristics of networked thinking and pursue a disciplined practice of certain principles embodied with that practice.

Key Characteristics of Networked Thinking

Networked thinking avoids getting stuck in old "object" associations. Driven by the mechanics of its Default system, our brain system's natural tendency is to associate an "object" with other objects as it always has. For example, in modern American culture, the Default system mechanics of an adult human brain system would normally associate the "object" of "success" with the "objects" of financial and social status, because it would have been bombarded for decades with memes that reinforced those associations. Networked thinking allows entirely new associations to be formed around the "object" of "success", perhaps connecting it with a certain sense of fulfillment, the respect of another person, or the feeling of having made a positive difference in the world.

Networked thinking also has a decidedly collective orientation and particular perspective on Theory of Mind. It is not oriented toward "either/or" determinations but seeks the "both/and" solutions that factor in both concerns centered on the self and the need for "public goods". In this way, it is non-linear, but at the same time, one of its primary aims is generating useful syntheses of information into knowledge. In the complex human brain system, there is no capacity for Bayesian updating without synthesis, and without Bayesian updating, there is no emergent intelligence.

Networked thinking is holistic but economical, focused on the message that needs to be communicated, while avoiding the "noise" that might obscure it. At the same time, it seeks out Random Information. It is open-minded and promotes curiosity, fascination, imagination, and ideation. It does not succumb to the Principle of Least Effort but optimizes the balance between effort and output value.

Networked thinking embraces tension as a source of opportunity for emergent creativity. It focuses on possibility and is not ruled by the human brain system's native aversion to loss and "failure". In fact, it embraces the notion that the human brain system and the emergent human mind essentially learn by trial and error. It is a common understanding within both neuroscience and psychology that the human brain system and mind "learn" more from their "mistakes" than from the predictions they get right. Networked thinking seeks to leverage this reality.

Networked thinking also consciously avoids other key heuristics and biases embedded in the human brain system, including:

- *Immediacy/clarity/availability*
  Networked thinking avoids the human brain system's propensity to prioritize information and ideas that are the most immediately available and unambiguous. Networked thinking pays attention to novel pieces of information but does not overvalue them.

- *Implicit association bias*
  Networked thinking involves high levels of self-awareness and is careful not to get sidetracked by our brain system's implicit association biases, especially those involving race and negative associations around morality or intelligence.
- *Affirmation bias*
  Networked thinking involves consciously avoiding the tendency of the human brain system to produce behaviors that will get noticed and be "affirmed" by members of an important social or professional group; quite the contrary, networked thinking seeks diversity of perspective and collective insight but is leery of "groupthink" and the effects of peer pressure.
- *Future/success bias*
  Networked thinking consciously avoids the bias of the human brain's Default system toward actions and behaviors that have been successful in the past. Simple statistical mechanics make it clear that thinking from extrapolation necessarily limits a wide range of possible outcomes, including those that did not occur in the past.

Key Practices of Networked Thinking

Because it involves new processes and seeks to break away from old mental habits, networked thinking requires the disciplined pursuit of certain practices:

1. Networked thinking requires the use of the entire brain, using the particular tools of the Integrated system, which encourages information flow between and among all the brain's functional systems, generating a highly integrated output.
2. Networked thinking requires an active, conscious, and intentional appreciation for how the human brain system operates as a complex adaptive system and is therefore highly influenced by the contents and choices of the mind. Meditation and other mindfulness exercises can help enable such a practice.
3. Networked thinking demands that we actually make a number of different mindful choices. Our brain/minds have *moment to moment* freedom of choice—the unfettered capacity to engage in self-reflectiveness consciousness and choose, in any given moment,

the *content* of our minds. These unfettered choices may be hard to sustain for very long, but the more we practice, the better our brain/mind become at self-analysis and self-reflection. And if we can choose the content of our minds at any given moment, we can certainly choose how to develop more enduring mindsets as well.

4. Networked thinking can be enhanced by practicing visualization. One of the elements that distinguishes the human brain system and its emergent mind from those of other animals is the capacity for visualization and imagination. The more time we spend visualizing how our Integrated system and its Small World information gathering and processing networks actually function, the more likely we are to take full advantage of its capacities. Also, according to research that links the dissipation of bad memories to neo-cortical feedback systems that are tightly connected to the amygdala, it seems that visualizing how that process works could help reduce one's tendency to get trapped in the negative suggestions of past experiences and extrapolate from those past experience when making predictions about the future. Finally, visualizing the types of three dimensional neural networks that self-organize in our brain systems and how information flows within them can make a difference in how they perform, just as visualizing the performance of physical activities like shooting a basketball free throw has been demonstrated to improve one's effectiveness in those activities.

5. Networked thinking also demands attention to the important memes that may be consciously or unconsciously invading our minds.

6. Network thinking requires that we understand the dynamics of our brain's reward systems and that we consciously choose the rewards that drive our decision making. That may sound simple, but it is not. Most people are in some way or another fooled into seeking rewards that either fail to satisfy the desires of their minds or fail to generate the "sense of reward" within key areas of the human brain system (amygdala, nucleus accumbens or lateral striatum) that are critical to sustaining motivation and delivering a sense of fulfillment.

Networked thinking can significantly change the content and focus of our minds, and ultimately the content and structures of our brain systems as well. Toward that end, we must always remember how critical repetition is to our brain systems generally. And just as our brain systems use the dynamics of LTP (long-term potentiation) to "strengthen" the synaptic connections within neural networks, so as to increase the speed and accuracy of such information processing networks, so also will the practice of networked thinking increase the "strength" of the networks they employ. When it comes to the human brain system, capacities of mind, and effectiveness of thought, it is all about practice, practice, practice.

9

NETWORKED THINKING IN ORGANIZATIONS:
THE "KNOWLEDGE NETWORK" AND OTHER
ORGANIZATIONAL DEVELOPMENT TOOLS

As powerful a tool as networked thinking is when practiced by a single person, its greatest utility may lie in how it can be deployed within a select, strategically designed network of people, in order to advance an organization's strategic thinking and development. In other words, properly designed networks of people, using the tools of networked thinking, may be able to share information and knowledge more effectively and generate better ideas than would be possible within traditional organizational structures, giving rise to a myriad of competitive advantages.

Studies undertaken by network scientists indicate that 1) the most common, and apparently most compelling, structure for personal networks is a triangle, and 2) the most effective networks for sharing information and knowledge contain a range of 12-18 people, of diverse backgrounds, functional knowledge, relationships/networks, personalities (pensive, gregarious, perspicacious, etc.), and professional strengths (analytical, visionary, good at "connecting people", optimist, champion, and so forth). Accordingly, the most stable, efficient, and effective design for this kind of network, which I will refer to as a "Knowledge Network", is a Small World structure of 3-5 triangular clusters, which are connected to a series of other strategic participants through 3-5 weak ties. In this chapter, I will focus primarily on how this type of Knowledge Network can be used as both a unique information processing tool and a model for efficient organizational development.

The human brain system traffics primarily in data (or Information, as per Information Theory), while the emergent human mind deals primarily with information patterns, which in some cases translate into knowledge. Similarly, Knowledge Networks in organizations are also designed to share patterns of information that can turn into valuable, often mission critical knowledge. The key issue in both cases is how to generate symmetry-breaking collective intelligence and wise decision-making while avoiding the symmetry-breaking behavior of "Groupthink". Both the human brain and the human organization are complex adaptive systems in which symmetry breaking collective behaviors and thinking emerge, but sometimes that collective thinking is brilliant, and sometimes it is stifling. Promoting the former and avoiding the latter can be a challenge.

I maintain that networked thinking is the way to address this challenge. By its nature, networked thinking is oriented toward open-ended, inclusive, and collaborative thinking. In its processes, networked thinking pursues Random Information, diversity of information, and consistent feedback. Properly structured Knowledge Networks in which the participants diligently practice networked thinking will generate collective intelligence where other organizational decision-making structures might ordinarily encourage Groupthink.

As noted in Chapter Three, network structural design has a major impact on how information flows and is processed. To optimize the effectiveness of a Knowledge Network, we will want to come up with a structure that both encourages the use of networked thinking and maximizes its facility for generating useful synthesis, shared knowledge, and innovative ideas. Some of the considerations that go into this structural design include the following:

- Knowledge Networks should use a Small World configuration, with the right number and structure of clusters, so that information and knowledge can be efficiently synthesized and fed forward into the rest of the network; weak ties should be created in such a way that the network will retain the right level of diversity, in terms of both information input and output (to other exogenous networks, information channels, etc.); the design of specific clusters within the Small World configuration should take into account issues such as the competence level of any given person in the cluster, as well as his or her formal or informal authority and any expectations regarding the directed or undirected nature of the communication links within the cluster.

- The most feasible professional network size has been demonstrated to consist of 10-14 people, so the design of Knowledge Networks within organizations should take that factor into account.
- Just as complex adaptive systems rely on the processing of both Random and Ordered Information to continue innovating and adapting, Knowledge Networks should do likewise; network design should take into account how information flows into and within the network and incorporate a predictive mechanism for identifying potentially useful Random Information.
- Just as complex adaptive systems generate emergent phenomena to create multiple levels of organization, each with its own information processing capabilities, Knowledge Networks should identify the emergent phenomena (e.g., culture of candor, trust, etc.) that will serve specific organizational functions, then design their network structures so as to promote and support the integrity of emergent phenomena.
- Knowledge Networks should design feedforward and feedback systems that 1) reinforce and support the sharing of information and knowledge, formulation of synthesis, and attainment of network goals, and 2) reinforce and support the emergent phenomena that are critical to organizational integrity (as suggested in the point above).

Small World Network Dynamics

Small World networks operate "cost efficiently" and create great information and knowledge sharing balance, while Scale Free communication network structures can concentrate too much power and influence in a single node or cluster. Small World networks encourage diversity of information input and continue to operate effectively even when a few nodes randomly go offline for a period, as usually happens in organizations where workloads and priorities fluctuate. No one person (node) in a Knowledge Network has to carry the burden of insuring that the right information and knowledge is reaching the right people in the network, although it is advisable for one person, or a particular cluster of people, depending on the size and scope of the Knowledge Network, to remain responsible for information and knowledge synthesis for the network.

The Small World structure also facilitates the task of identifying and arranging the right mix of participants, based on their professional expertise, competence with information and knowledge sharing, formal and informal position of authority within the organization, and dedication to the Knowledge Network concept. Some people perceive the value of information and knowledge more than others, some are naturally more collaborative than others, and some are just more social and responsive than others. It takes the right mix of personalities, passion for learning, cultural legacies, and the like to build an effective Knowledge Network, and Small World network structures make it easier to design and implement an appropriate combination of participants.

Additionally, the Small World structure will optimize the value of the participants' personal and professional networks, which are by definition tied into the Knowledge Network by weak, directed ties. Subject to the discretion necessary in protecting the integrity of the Knowledge Network, participants can use their own personal and professional networks to source potentially useful Random Information, seek diversity of input, and tap into different kinds of information distribution networks, all without adversely affecting the structural dynamics and operational integrity of the Knowledge Network itself.

Random and Ordered Information

Random Information is critical to the emergence of innovation within a Knowledge Network. Ordered Information, on the other hand, holds the keys to "rules" of statistical accumulation that dictate how new information will be processed within the Knowledge Network, if at all. These predictive "rules" need to be constantly updated by and through the ongoing synthesis of shared knowledge within the network.

For example, suppose a Knowledge Network of 10 professionals within an American healthcare products company (not necessarily its "executives"!) were formed into two distinct but linked clusters of three people, with one cluster containing a market research analyst, product design expert, and customer service representative, and the other being comprised of a graphic artist, organic chemist, and designated "networked thinker". The two clusters are also separately linked, through a series of weak ties, with four other people, namely the CEO, CFO, a marketing consultant living in Paris, and the stay at home husband of a middle manager in the Human Resources department. The company's goal is to position itself as the market leader in the design, manufacture, and delivery of moderately priced healthcare products that use only natural ingredients that can be proven to have zero negative side effects.

The market research analyst has been combing the globe for natural ingredients that are not native to the U.S., checking in occasionally with the organic chemist who is part of the other cluster in the Knowledge Network. Together they begin to find organic compounds that seem linked by a particular Information pattern. Using statistical accumulation tools, they synthesize that information and "feed it forward" into the Knowledge Network. Shortly thereafter, the stay at home husband emails back that he got the message and became curious, so he went into the kids' bathroom and looked at the label of a French shampoo his wife had bought for the kids, after he had noticed the day before that his four year old daughter's hair had looked exceptionally vibrant after using the shampoo. In the email, he lists the ingredients of the shampoo, which the organic chemist later determines share a chemical Information pattern with the synthesized information transmitted in the original email. The same day the CEO replies to the original email, stating that the company board wants to significantly expand its product line, so he is interested in hearing more about this research.

No doubt the research analyst and product development expert ratchet up their sense of urgency after reading the CEO's email, and fortunately the serendipitous bits of information shared by the stay at home husband turn out to be some very fortuitous Random Information, which provides them with new impetus. Maybe they are even able to design some genetic algorithms that will take the Random Information and produce a set of Information patterns that give rise to a new chemical composition that not only improves the condition of normal hair but minimizes hair loss. Additional synthesis of the existing information sets may provide predictive clues about where to find other naturally occurring chemical compounds that can also be factored into the company's product design genetic algorithms. Perhaps even the "rules" embedded in those algorithms, or other product design processes, are updated by the newly synthesized information, which leads to adjustments of the Knowledge Network's Ordered Information and operating premises.

This example clearly demonstrates not only the dynamic nature of information and knowledge sharing in Knowledge Networks but the significance of predictive mechanisms. The more a participant in the

Knowledge Network knows, the better he or she is able to communicate both Random Information and relevant knowledge; the more Random Information and relevant knowledge, the more useful the synthesis; the more useful the synthesis, the better the predictive models and the more facile all Knowledge Network participants will become with the mechanics of an effective information sharing network.

Emergent phenomena and their effect on information sharing in networks

One of the fascinating aspects of the human brain system as a complex adaptive system is what emerges from its intricate information sharing networks in the form of mind, thinking, memory, knowledge, wisdom, and intelligence. In like fashion, it seems entirely reasonable that a well-designed Knowledge Network would also be able to generate some significant emergent phenomena and properties. There is no reason why a Knowledge Network would not be able to convert synthesized knowledge into a collective wisdom, cumulative intelligence into strategic thinking, or specialized talents into "public goods". Moreover, Knowledge Networks are capable of developing emergent *properties*, such as conventions for responsiveness to requests for information or knowledge, high levels of goodwill and trust, or contagious curiosity.

For example, suppose a hospital organized a Knowledge Network to help it develop new ideas and better strategies for patient care. Given that hospitals are always accommodating not only patients and their families but other professionals who are not employees, such as clergy, salespeople, and consultants, such a Knowledge Network might be connected by weak ties to people who, while not employees, still need to comply with important rules and regulations, especially HIPAA. Trust and cooperation would be a major concern, not only for the hospital organization itself but the Knowledge Network that is operating inside it.

As we noted in the last chapter, however, all these emergent phenomena and properties operate at their own organizational level, with varying degrees of predictability. You cannot predict what a given person's mind is like by analyzing his brain system, and you cannot predict what he is thinking by investigating the nature of his mind. Likewise, you cannot predict what level of cooperation will emerge just by looking at the structure of a Knowledge Network, and you cannot predict how any one network participant will respond in any given situation just by analyzing the general level of cooperation within the network. So the best way for the hospital to not only promote the effectiveness of the Knowledge Network but also safeguard against the potential mishandling or leaking of information within that network is to build a solid foundation of trust and trustworthiness, ethical behavior, and attention to detail.

For an organization like a hospital this is critically important, because the potential risk of mishandled or leaked information should not be allowed to threaten the prospective benefits of a Knowledge Network. The Knowledge Network offers too much upside, in the form of the wisdom that can be gained on how to proactively address patient health; the development of better strategies for operational policies, such as instituting new handwashing procedures or other preventive measures for reducing the circulation of infection; or the production of evidence based protocols for deciding dilemmas, such as whether a patient should be admitted or held for observation in the Emergency Department. Like many organizations, hospital administrations are not set up to innovatively explore many of the pressing operational issues that Knowledge Networks can creatively address.

There is a wide range of network dynamics that affect the emergence of key network phenomena such as trust, goodwill, and collaboration, which in turn will either enhance or impede the flow of data, information, or knowledge within a Knowledge Network. For example, in a professional network of doctors, each participant will have different 1) training and expertise, 2) intelligence (including social and emotional intelligence), 3) personality and reputation, 4) communication style, 5) cultural legacy, values, perspectives, and perceptions, and 6) motivations and inclinations to collaborate, all of which will affect their level of participation in some form or another. Additionally, based on the type of information flowing through the network, as well as collateral issues such as time constraints or professional jealousies, each of the "links" (read, relationships between the doctors) will produce varying levels of reciprocity. As the network goes into operation, each doctor will begin to generate a history of link traffic (personal and professional doctor interaction) that may not only influence the existing degrees of link reciprocity but perhaps even change the structure of the network itself, thereby altering its dynamics.

Not that impedance to information flow is always a bad thing. Just as electrical circuits require designed impedance to complete certain functions and brains need inhibitory neurons to regulate synaptic activity,

Knowledge Networks must use various types of circuit-breakers and governors to manage the flow of information and protect their integrity. As we know, if there is too much "noise" in the network, the relevant messages and critical pieces of Random Information will get lost in the mix. If too much information flows through the "pipeline", network nodes will be overwhelmed.

Feedforward and feedback systems that generate synthesis

Knowledge Networks are personal—they involve all the vagaries of human thought and behavior. Humans fall prey to the mechanics and thoughts generated by the Default system; they get locked into patterns of thought; they make predictions simply by extrapolating from the past. Given this reality, Knowledge Networks must have designed into them dedicated feedforward and feedback systems that alter the default behaviors of humans and institute robust information and knowledge sharing dynamics.

Feedforward systems are necessary to remind network participants of its goals and objectives, keep them focused. Feedback systems are necessary to modulate default thoughts and behaviors, then recalibrate them to the task at hand. Moreover, just as they serve the human brain/mind in testing and updating their predictions, feedforward and feedback systems in Knowledge Networks generate valuable insights and new perspectives on the objectives being pursued within the Knowledge Network. Feedforward and feedback systems can also be used in Knowledge Networks to direct subject matter focus. We understand implicitly how to direct our time and attention to specific tasks on which we are asked by colleagues to collaborate, but we generally have no effective way of doing so with a group of people with whom we have no "operating history". As pointed out in Chapter Three, one of the key characteristics of a network is its operation history, because of how that informs the network's information sharing dynamics going forward; certainly, over time, feedback systems in a Knowledge Network would help to create this kind of rich operating history.

Knowledge Network connections to the outside world

One of the most compelling aspects of any network lies in the dynamics of its reach. While complex systems revolve around the dynamics of relationships and are necessarily subject to boundary limitations, no such limitation exists with networks. Weak ties can extend a personal, social, or professional network from one side of the globe to the other in but a few degrees of distribution.

Because Knowledge Networks thrive on diversity of information input and feedback, it is important to strategically design a Knowledge Network's connections to the "outside world". In some cases, that "outside world" might mean include a professional contact in a different but idea rich cultural environment; in others, it might mean connecting to an "outside the box thinker" who lives right next door and is known for how consistently he is able to look at patterns of information from a unique angle. The point is to achieve a *strategic* diversity of information input.

In designing the connections of a Knowledge Network to the outside world, it is important to keep in mind the many different cultural, professional, and personal predilections people carry with them and often manifest in their communication styles. Generally, a Knowledge Network requires high levels of responsiveness, both in timeliness and thoughtfulness, so it is important to factor that element into the equation when determining what type of weak ties to form between a Knowledge Network and individuals outside the network.

Of course, some connections (links) to the outside world are more useful than others. Professional reputation, credentials, even the quality of a person's written or oral communication can all affect the value of information and knowledge sharing from such connections. People are disinclined to share their knowledge when they do not think they are going to receive significant value in return—human social and professional coherence are fundamentally premised on cooperation and collaboration. Actual or perceived authority of potential contributors matters as well. For example, LinkedIn Groups tries to categorize certain members as "top contributors", presumably in an attempt to not only encourage them to keep starting conversations and contributing their insights, but also to encourage them to share their knowledge with other members and get more of those members to either contribute more or recruit new members in the future.

Moreover, people in a professional or social network bent on sharing information or knowledge will inevitably be affected by formal or informal power structures and other forms of actual or implied influence. A network embedded in a Congressional caucus, for example, will likely be driven in large measure by the dynamics of how different congressmen and congresswomen

149

have voted on bills, how lobbyists have pressed their business within the caucus, and other exigencies surrounding the power and influence subtleties of life Inside the Beltway. Of course, these factors can vary from culture to culture, and phenomena such as "power distance", which is the measure of how much people defer to actual or perceived power, can make a huge difference in the dynamics of a professional network. In Africa, for example, people in political or military power are generally accorded maximum perceived authority, whereas in America, even the President is sometimes regarded as someone whose knowledge and intelligence may not even measure up to the gravitas of a neighbor down the street.

It bears reiteration that personality and other psychological factors such as emotional and social intelligence have significant impacts on the operational dynamics of a professional network, including a Knowledge Network, primarily because of their potential "cascading" effect within the network. Network science has demonstrated that the emergent phenomenon of "percolation"—which results from the strong connections people make with each other over common personality traits, interests, and the like—leads to the self-organization of clusters based on individual preferences and characteristics. Percolation in turn adds an element of "viral spreading" dynamics, which can be both useful and dangerous to organizations, depending on whether it results in cascading success or failure. Moreover, viral spreading and cascading dynamics are accentuated by the presence of people who act as "Connectors". Research shows that social and professional networks usually "center" around small groups/clusters of influential people, and clearly the presence of high trust levels within a network contributes to the strengthening of links between these centers and all the other network nodes.

The Knowledge Network's connections to useful external networks need not be limited to personal ones—the Internet and the Web are also vital to the success of a Knowledge Network. The Internet provides a stable Small World network structure that makes possible the self-organizing, Scale Free network that is the Web, which in turn makes it possible to find all manner of distributed intelligence throughout the globe. The Web is also an invaluable source of historical information on the emergence, variation, and spreading of memes. The trillions of pages that are linked together on the Web create a distributed network of networks, much like the human brain system's information processing system. And much like the human brain system's neural networks, these Web links are constantly representing, cataloguing, and associating "objects", which leads to the emergence of ideas that can quickly become memes if they involve some aspect of human behavior that can be easily imitated.

The Web may even provide a source of *original* intelligence to Knowledge Networks. Given their similar structures and methods of cataloguing and manipulating "objects", the Web forms a natural link with the human brain system and offers the possibility that millions of networked human brain systems could generate the type of parallel processing power that could give rise to a whole new level of intelligence—human artificial, and or some combination of the two. Of course, the emergence of such intelligence would require a sophisticated network of *undirected* links. Most blogs and "free speech" sites like Twitter involve *directed* links that are lacking in true mutuality of information and knowledge exchange.

Implementing Knowledge Networks in organizations

I started this book by making some distinctions between what is "complex" in our lives and what is "complicated". Without a doubt, one of the major reasons that our 21st century lives are both complex and complicated stems from the shift that is taking place in our relationship to information. One might even say that we are moving from an "Information Era" to a "Knowledge Era". ("Knowledge" in this context is best described as the understanding of how to most efficiently and effectively apply information in a given situation—what we might call "smart information" or "applied information".) With the advent of the Internet, private intranets, and other communication systems advances, information has become easily accessible and distributable. But not all information is created equal, so on the one hand we are being overwhelmed by the sheer volume of information in our lives, and on the other we are having difficulty figuring out what information is relevant and useful to enhancing our knowledge, and what information should simply be ignored. In other words, when information is easily available, knowledge becomes more valuable, which suggests that now more than ever we need the strategic benefits of Knowledge Networks, particularly within our organizations.

Our organizations have an urgent need for information that directly feeds their strategic decision making. Big data can be crunched into information that provides only a few slices of customers' psychographic and behavioral profiles. At the other end of the spectrum, firms collect phenomenological information on customer behaviors but can only manage to engage in this kind of research with hundreds of such customers rather than millions. Data we have, but there is still a big gap between the nature and amount of information that organizations are collecting and that which is required to reduce market uncertainties and facilitate effective product/service design, marketing, and sales strategies. Knowledge Networks can address that information gap.

Add to this the fact that we operate today in the commerce of ideas, expressed through the filter of increasing specialization. To succeed, organizations will have to get better at sharing information and knowledge WHEN and WHERE they are needed. Strategically engineering WHEN and WHERE commands is what makes Artificial Intelligence possible, yet no communication network outside the human brain system has been able to master the challenge of programming these commands into a system that delivers information and knowledge where it is needed, at the precise moment it is needed. You can get your Twitter feeds sent to your phone, but they will not consistently show up when you have the time to read them or absorb the information in them. Properly constructed and managed, Knowledge Networks can begin to generate their own embedded WHEN and WHERE commands, allowing for the timely deployment of knowledge throughout the organization.

Knowledge Networks will also help organizations deliver and share *experiential* knowledge. Today, our brain systems and minds have gotten used to plugging into directed networks that "push" information and limited knowledge at us, and over time we have come to think that the knowledge we need is available through these channels. We expect to manage all our short-term learning by "Googling" the applicable subject matter. But the truth is that experience does count, and just as in the past you could not learn how to practice law or medicine, trade securities, or run a company simply by reading a book, you also cannot do so by listening to someone explain it to you in a webinar. Knowledge Networks allows for the sharing of experiential knowledge that goes beyond such "push" learning processes, because they have embedded in then an expectation that information and knowledge is always being synthesized, applied toward specific goals, and directed at generating critical new "ideas".

Knowledge Networks also serve an important role in identifying the memes that flow through an organization, then sorting them and choosing which ones to spread, which to stop. Memes that contribute to and reinforce organizational values and culture can make the difference between success and failure, and very likely the same is true with memes that work at cross purposes to such values and culture. Well-designed and focused Knowledge Networks can even engineer the adoption and spreading of memeplexes (an integrated collection of related memes), whose reinforcing influences may in some cases exponentially increase the benefits that accrue across the organization.

Knowledge Networks can make organizations better at predictive analysis. Obviously, predictive analysis depends on feedback systems of one sort or another, and in most organizations, feedback systems become quickly diluted and remain largely ineffective. By focusing this feedback process in smaller, dedicated communications networks like a Knowledge Network, an organization can begin to establish a mindset and culture that highlight the importance of feedback mechanisms.

Implementing a Knowledge Network (KN) within an organization can provide the following benefits:

1. Promoting networked thinking among KN participants
2. Designing the KN so that there are clusters that are responsible for generating certain types of information, knowledge, synthesis, new ideas, and feedforward messaging
3. Designing the proper weak ties into the KN to provide necessary Random Information, perspective diversity, and feedback
4. Insuring that information and knowledge synthesis is messaged using the proper Shannon Information balance between signal and noise
5. Integrating the KN with the appropriate dynamics of the organization's reward system
6. Strategically updating predictive models

Most people would probably like to make their lives less complex and complicated, if they were able. But the same is not true for an organization, which is its own kind of complex adaptive system and therefore needs to embrace the ever-increasing complexity that is implicit in the self-organization of information within our modern world. Fortunately, organizations are powered by humans, and we are great processors of information. But as complexity continues to increase, organizations must become increasingly efficient in the way they process information, add value, and grow. Knowledge Networks are essential to consistently achieving each of these goals and to generating the ideas and tactics that deliver effective organizational development strategies.

www.ingramcontent.com/pod-product-compliance
Lightning Source LLC
Chambersburg PA
CBHW080810180526
45168CB00006B/2392